101st U.S. Open Championship
Southern Hills Country Club
June 14-18, 2001

ISBN 1-878843-32-X

©2001 United States Golf Association®
Golf House, Far Hills, N.J. 07931

Statistics produced by Unisys Corporation

Photographs on pages 60-63 by Allsport
Course photography by Fred Vuich
Course illustrations by Dan Wardlaw © The Majors of Golf

Published by IMG Worldwide Inc.,
1360 East Ninth Street, Cleveland, Ohio 44114

Designed and produced by Davis Design

Printed in the United States of America

It has often been said that you don't win United States Open Championships. Somebody loses them. That is certainly not always the case — take Tiger Woods' 15-stroke victory at Pebble Beach in 2000 or perhaps the way I won in 1960 at Cherry Hills — but that surely seemed to be what was happening late Sunday afternoon at Southern Hills in 2001. What a strange set of circumstances! Unprecedented in the storied history of the Open.

All due credit should go to Retief Goosen, though, for swallowing the bitter pill of missing the winning putt after leading the field for three rounds and recovering the next day to win the championship. Goosen, little known in the U.S. but a solid player for years on the European and South African Tours, may well go on to a productive career on the PGA Tour. Winning the Open laid out the welcome mat for him for every tournament in which he wants to play, taking the dreaded word *qualify* out of his golfing vocabulary for many years to come, if not forever.

This annual publication that chronicles each U.S. Open in detailed words and photographs not only portrays the bizarre finish at Southern Hills, but also deals with the other sub-plots that ensued in the steamy heat of Tulsa. It follows the play of Tiger Woods and the others, like David Duval and Phil Mickelson, who were given the best chances of winning the championship. Woods, the defending champion, whose record streak of four consecutive victories in the game's major championships began with the resounding victory at Pebble Beach and ended at Southern Hills, never recovered fully from a poor opening round.

Reminisce and enjoy this 17th annual commemorative book presented by Rolex and the United States Golf Association.

Arnold Palmer

The second hole, par 4 and 467 yards.

Looking back to 1936:
Germany invaded the Rhineland, violating the Versailles Treaty and taking the first step leading to the Second World War; Franklin Roosevelt won 46 of the 48 states and smothered Alfred M. Landon in the presidential election; and Bruno Richard Hauptmann was executed for the kidnapping and murder of the Lindbergh baby. Jesse Owens won four gold medals in the Olympics; Tony Manero shaved four strokes off the Open scoring record, shooting 282 at Baltusrol Golf Club; and Joe DiMaggio played his first season with the Yankees.

And millions suffered as the world sank deeper into the Great Depression. The American Southwest suffered with everyone else. Trapped in the devastating drought that caused the dust bowl, desperate families fled Oklahoma for California and found not the promised land but more despair.

Against this backdrop, 29 men met in Tulsa and played the first round of golf at the Southern Hills Country Club. They may well have opened the finest golf course in the mid-continent. It is certainly among the nation's most unusual, not so much because it is among the game's finest examinations, but that it exists at all ranks as the wonder of the times. It was the product of generosity, determination and a gifted golf course designer.

Tulsa sits in the northeastern corner of Oklahoma. Originally a post office on the Pony Express mail route, Tulsey Town later became a shipping center for cattle headed for the stockyards of St. Louis and Chicago on the Atlantic and Pacific Railroad. But when the railroad shifted its terminal a few miles south, Tulsa nearly disappeared. Then, in 1901, a wildcatter brought in a well across the Arkansas River, and the city grew into a center of world oil production.

Sensing the opportunity of a lifetime, the Phillips family jumped into the oil business and prospered, creating the Phillips Petroleum Company (its Phillips 66 gasoline stations dot roadsides throughout the West). Waite Phillips became the key man of Southern Hills.

Early in the 1930s, as the economic agony deepened, rumors circulated that the Tulsa Country Club was about to turn its course into a public facility. It was a baseless scare, but it galvanized a group of golfers into approaching Phillips about land he owned southeast of town. They were ambitious. They asked if he would give them 300 acres so they could build a club with an Olympic-size swimming pool, stables and bridle paths, tennis courts, a polo field, skeet range, a clubhouse and a golf course.

Asking for free land took some nerve, but they knew their man. Phillips agreed, but he laid down difficult terms.

First, they would have to raise $150,000 to finance the club.

Second, they had 18 days to do it.

This was a time, of course, when someone said, money was "scarcer than dinosaur bones." No one had much, but somehow, within the time limit, 140 potential members pledged $140,000. It didn't quite meet Phillips' mandate, but he felt it was close enough.

Construction crews began work in 1933 and completed the job in 1935, a period of U.S. history when perhaps the only other new courses were built for municipalities, using hand labor and financed with federal funds under either the Public Works Administration (PWA) or the Works Progress Administration (WPA), a make-work project set up to create jobs for the massive number of unemployed, which had reached 20 percent.

By then, golf had hit rock bottom throughout the world. The British Open, the most cosmopolitan of the great events, had drawn steady streams of players from the U.S. since the end of the First World War, but with money drying up, hardly anyone could afford the trip, and the championship settled into relative decline.

Meantime, clubs in the United States were abandoned faster than they had opened. In 1930, the year after the Wall Street collapse, the United States Golf Association listed 1,134 member clubs; by 1935, the roll had shrunk to 767.

In this gloomy climate, these strong-willed, optimistic Oklahomans created their club. That they managed is an improbable success story, but the prominence of the golf course is owed to Perry Maxwell.

When he agreed to turn over the land, Phillips suggested the group hire Maxwell, an old friend, to lay out the golf course. Taken as a command, the suggestion may have been as valuable as the land he had donated, for Maxwell designed one of the game's jewels.

Born in Kentucky, Maxwell had settled in Oklahoma in 1900, when it was still Indian Territory (the state's name is a combination of two Choctaw words that together mean red people). An educated man — valedictorian of his graduating class at the University of Kentucky — he went into banking, rose to vice president and was elected to a seat on the board of directors of the Ardmore National Bank, became a wealthy man, and gave it up when he turned 40. An enthusiastic golfer, he had built a nine-hole course near Ardmore, a few miles north of the Red River, which separates Oklahoma from Texas. In a fit of whimsy he named it Dornick Hills. In Gaelic, the word dornick means small rocks, evidently a commentary on the land he had to work with.

As word spread about the quality of Southern Hills, Maxwell's reputation grew, and he was given other major assignments. He laid out the first nine of Prairie Dunes Country Club in Hutchinson, Kan. (His son, Press, did the second nine.) He did some work on Pine Valley Golf Club, and Bob Jones asked him to improve a few holes at Augusta National. He revised the seventh and moved the 10th green from its original position alongside the big fairway bunker to the top of the hill 40 to 50 yards beyond, setting up a

1st
PAR 4
454 YARDS

2nd
PAR 4
467 YARDS

3rd
PAR 4
408 YARDS

The fourth hole, par 4 and 368 yards.

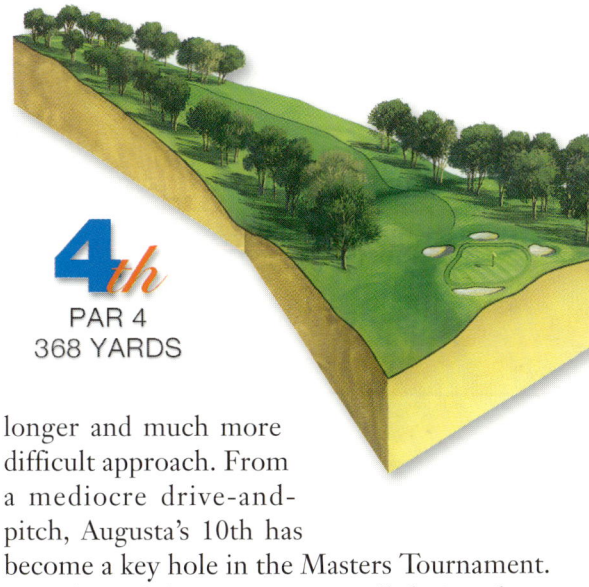

4th
PAR 4
368 YARDS

longer and much more difficult approach. From a mediocre drive-and-pitch, Augusta's 10th has become a key hole in the Masters Tournament.

Through his career, Maxwell designed more than 70 courses and revised about 50 others. Still, he will always be remembered for Southern Hills.

He lived by the philosophy that the man who builds a golf course should take what the land offers. Working without topographic maps, he walked the ground carrying a sketch pad. Then he shaped the land with mule teams pulling drag pans, the same technique Donald Ross used building Pinehurst No. 2.

Looking outwards from the long, low, white clubhouse sitting at the crest of the only real hill in the region, the tall buildings of modern Tulsa rise above the trees. The course begins on this hill, then drops sharply to rolling ground.

There it swings off to the left for the first nine, turns back to the clubhouse, then angles to the right for the second nine, ending with a steep climb back up the hill for the rugged closing hole, a 466-yard par 4 with an elevated green and a tight opening guarded by deep bunkers left and right.

To conquer Southern Hills, the golfer must master a variety of shots — long irons, short irons, pitches, chips and the occasional fairway wood, because this is no monotonous slog through an endless series of backbreaking 475-yard par 4s. Five of its par-4 holes measure less than 400 yards. The longest of these, the seventh, stretches no more than 382 yards, and the 17th measures 365 yards.

Southern Hills

The seventh hole, par 4 and 382 yards.

5th
PAR 5
642 YARDS

Yet no one tore them apart.

Tiger Woods never could handle the ninth, at 374 yards no more than a sand-iron second for him. At the end of his four rounds it had cost him four strokes — a double-bogey 6 in the first round, and bogey 5s in the third and fourth.

Only a few of its driving holes run straight from tee to green. The others bend either right or left, some mildly, some wildly, as they weave among canopies of oak, hackberry, a variety of elm, and a few scattered sycamore, maple and cottonwood trees.

Some holes gave the field fits. The second looks innocent enough, a par 4 of 467 yards, eminently reachable with modern equipment, but a creek cuts across from left to right, then purls along the left for a short distance.

Standing near the drive zone for any time, spectators ducked as balls clattered among tree branches or leaped aside as they splashed into the water hazard. Strangely, the second claimed 12 more scores of two over par or worse than the 18th, the most difficult hole to par.

It certainly impressed Clark Dennis, a 35-year-old Texan playing in his fifth Open.

"It's really a tight drive," he moaned. "You have the creek on the left and the trees on the right. To have that tough a hole that early in the round really stuck out. I mean, the second drive of the day! It really gets your attention."

The third swings sharply left, the fourth runs straight for 368 yards, and then a path leads up a gentle incline to the fifth, the most talked about hole on an Open course in some years.

It had always been a long hole; it measured 592 yards for the 1958 Open, and 614 yards for both the 1977 Open and 1994 PGA Championship. For this year's Open, the USGA marched another 28 yards farther back and built a new tee. At 642 yards, the fifth at Southern Hills supplanted the 17th at Baltusrol as the longest hole not only in the Open but in all of championship golf.

Not only was the hole exceptionally long, the drive had to find a target just 30 yards wide and settle where the fairway veers left to open a clear path to the green. Still, the fifth was reachable with the second shot.

6th
PAR 3
175 YARDS

7th
PAR 4
382 YARDS

Southern Hills

The 10th hole, par 4 and 374 yards.

The second nine turns away from the clubhouse, down another slope and around a left-to-right dogleg to the 10th green, a hole that, although short at 374 yards, cost Mark Brooks dearly in the playoff. Choosing to play his tee shot over towering trees at the corner of the dogleg, he drove into the rough, missed the green and bogeyed. Retief Goosen birdied. The two-stroke swing dropped Brooks five behind, strokes he wouldn't make up.

Past the 11th, at 165 yards the shortest of the par 3s, Southern Hills moves on to the 12th, an absolute gem. A beautifully designed par 4, it begins close to the club's boundary, runs straight for a time, then bends left, turning at a precisely placed fairway bunker. The green sits slightly below the drive zone, protected by bunkers on the left and a creek on the right. A great many players believe this is among the finest par-4 holes in the game.

From a new tee set about as far back as it could go, the 12th measures 456 yards and calls for two immaculate shots. The drive must thread a fairway drawn in to 26 yards and clear the corner of the right-to-left dogleg. The more powerful hitters can fly their drive over a bunker set where the fairway swings left, but it takes a carry of 275 yards.

Played from a downhill lie, the approach must avoid the bunker and the creek and find the flatish green. It is a classic hole.

It was not solely the work of Perry Maxwell.

While Maxwell was still working on the routing, Don Bothwell, one of the members, frequently walked the grounds with him and occasionally with John Winters, another member, clearing a patch of ground where Maxwell might suggest and drive or play approach shots. Testing the 12th one afternoon, both Winters, a tall man who hit the ball far, and Bothwell set themselves to play to the green, which Maxwell had placed where the 13th tee is today.

Not as long as Winters, Bothwell fretted about the length of the shot and asked Maxwell, "Why don't you put the green behind that creek down there?" pointing to a level patch behind a stream.

Maxwell looked at where Bothwell had pointed, then at where he had planned it. His eyes widened, and he cried, "Why didn't I see that?"

It was an inspired choice, not so much because the 12th is difficult, although it ranked as the fourth hardest to par, but because it plays so well and has such aesthetic appeal.

The 18th, on the other hand, is just tough. Speaking after a few practice rounds, Phil Mickelson described what he saw as the problems.

"The difficulties on 18 are three-fold," he explained. "You're hitting your second shot with a long iron. You're hitting your second shot from a downslope. You're hitting your second shot out of a tight lie. To hit the ball high enough off a skinny lie with a 2- or 3-iron is going to be very difficult.

"It plays a good club-and-a-half or two clubs longer than the yardage says, so it's a hole where you don't even think about a 3. You want to make a 4 and get out of there."

8th
PAR 3
225 YARDS

9th
PAR 4
374 YARDS

every green and planted a new strain of heat-resistant bentgrass that could be cut shorter and putt faster. Unfortunately, the ninth and 18th putted too fast.

Late Monday afternoon, Woods tested the ninth, putting from the back to the front. No matter how lightly he tapped the ball, most putts skidded off the front.

Actually, the 18th green had always been fast. Back in 1977, P.J. Boatwright Jr., the USGA's executive director, dropped a ball on the back of the green. For 21 seconds it rolled ever so slowly but steadily until it

It was also controversial.

Maxwell built lots of subtle contours into his greens, but the dips and rises of the ninth and 18th, which stand side-by-side, don't qualify as subtle. They are severe. During early practice rounds, shot after shot that carried to those greens paused if they didn't reach the back, then turned and tumbled down the hill. Players shook their heads and wondered what the USGA would do about it.

It wasn't supposed to be that way. After serious vandalism two years earlier, the club rebuilt

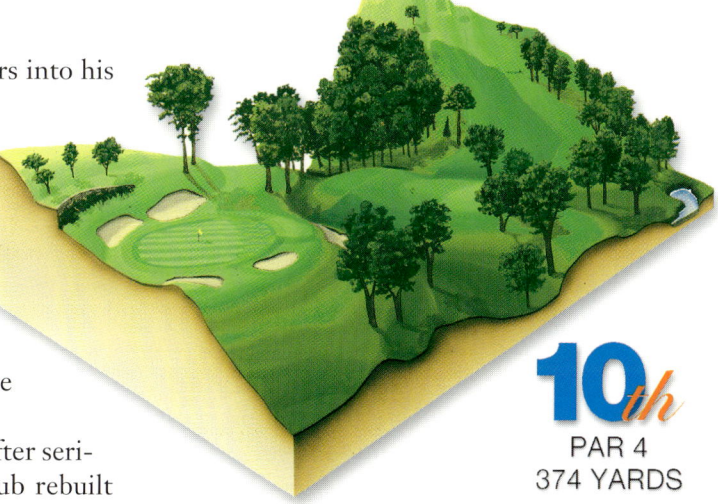

10th
PAR 4
374 YARDS

Southern Hills

trickled onto the fairway.

Tim Moraghan, the USGA's championship agronomist, solved the problem by allowing the grass on both those greens to grow slightly higher than on the others. Where the USGA aimed for Stimpmeter speeds of 11 to 11½ feet on the other 16 greens, the ninth and 18th would roll a foot slower. It all worked out.

At 6,973 yards, as it was set up for the Open, Southern Hills asked for no more than moderate length, but it demanded above all that the ball land where it was aimed. The cramped fairways ranged from a stingy 24 yards wide at the shortish fourth to 36 yards at the 18th, which ranks among the most difficult of all the Open finishing holes.

Players who missed their targets paid a heavy price. Unyielding bermudagrass rough, patchy in places, bordered every fairway, so dense it could rip the club from their hands.

After pulling their drives, both Tom Lehman and the Englishman Lee Westwood, two of the strongest men in the field, could only chop out short of the fourth green the first day. Remember, the fourth measures only 368 yards.

As a further mental hazard, trees planted as saplings 70 years ago had matured and had to be dealt with on nearly every hole.

11th
PAR 3
165 YARDS

12th
PAR 4
456 YARDS

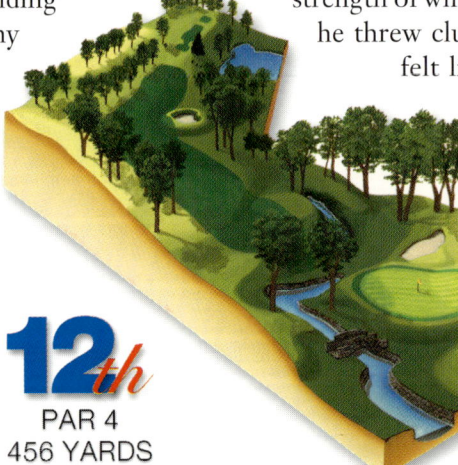

Following the pattern of the previous two Opens at Southern Hills, the 2001 championship packed at least as much drama into its four rounds — and the playoff.

In the 1958 Open, Tommy Bolt played nearly flawless golf and shot rounds of 71-71-69-72–283 to win by four strokes over Gary Player, a 22-year-old South African playing his second season on the U.S. tour. Player shot 287, two strokes better than Julius Boros. It seemed a strange twist of fate that Player had done so well in 1958 and Retief Goosen, another South African, had won 43 years later.

Like Ben Hogan, Bolt had blossomed late. He didn't play the tour successfully until he reached 30, but by then he had became a marvelous striker of the ball. He could drive with anyone, and he played stunning long irons.

Bolt had one glaring weakness. He lacked the strength of will to control his temper. At his worst he threw clubs, swore and insulted anyone he felt like insulting. At his best he could charm the warts off a frog. And he had a sense of humor.

On the morning of the Open's second round, a Tulsa newspaper reported his age as 49. Claiming to be 39, Bolt challenged the reporter during a press conference. The exchange has grown into Open lore.

"It was a typographical error, Tommy," the reporter said.

"Typographical error, hell," Bolt roared. "It

101st U.S. Open

The 12th hole, par 4 and 456 yards.

was a perfect four and a perfect nine."

It was all in fun; the small group of writers roared and Tommy smiled. He should have; born in 1916, he was actually 42.

His behavior that day should have given everyone a clue that Bolt somehow had found an inner peace. His nerves calm, he played golf as he had never played on any important occasion.

He couldn't have played the 12th hole better. It was said to have measured 465 yards in 1958, but it must have been shorter. Preparing for the 2001 Open, the club pushed the tee so far back the players nearly brushed against the chain-link fence that defines the club's borders. From this new tee it measured 456 yards; it was probably 20 yards shorter in 1958 and 1977.

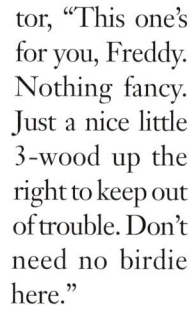

13th
PAR 5
534 YARDS

tor, "This one's for you, Freddy. Nothing fancy. Just a nice little 3-wood up the right to keep out of trouble. Don't need no birdie here."

"Just get it off the ground, Tommy," Freddy called back.

"Ain't this something?" Bolt said to Dan Jenkins, with the *Fort Worth Star-Telegram* then, "Old Tom's gonna win hisse'f a Ben Hogan kind of tournament. How about that, Pard!"

And he did, indeed.

Nineteen years later, Hubert Green had to overcome a situation more menacing than Tommy Bolt's temper. This was an Open remembered less for the quality of the golf than for its unusual circumstances.

With 18 holes to play under Tulsa's usually searing June heat, Green stood two strokes under par, just one stroke ahead of Andy Bean. They were paired together in the last round, and as they drove from the 10th tee, a Tulsa police lieutenant was telling the USGA a chilling story. A frantic woman had called the Oklahoma City office of the FBI claiming three men were on their way to Southern Hills to kill Green as he played the 15th hole.

The meeting was kept secret, but a phalanx of policemen suddenly appeared around

14th
PAR 3
215 YARDS

Drilling 3-irons into the green every day, Bolt played this trying hole with three birdies and surrendered to par only in the last round, when he had the championship in his possession. Hogan, on the other hand, double-bogeyed in the first round and bogeyed in the last. At the end, Bolt beat him by 11 strokes, six of those strokes on this hole alone.

With only a few holes left, a gaggle of writers streamed out to the 16th to watch Old Tom wrap it up. Tommy loved it.

Stepping up to his ball, he called to an old tormen-

15th
PAR 4
412 YARDS

101st U.S. Open

The 15th hole, par 4 and 412 yards.

Southern Hills

Green, the clubhouse was sealed off, policemen in plain clothes patrolled the gallery, and detectives climbed into the ABC television network's control trailer and gave orders to Roone Arledge, the president of ABC Sports, and Chuck Howard, who was producing the telecast.

Arledge and Howard were told to use cameras not actually showing the golf to scan the gallery and nearby rooftops by the 15th.

Green obviously had to be told, and he was already playing shaky golf. He had bogeyed the ninth and 10th, and now Lou Graham, the 1975 champion, was closing in. Losing ground with an outward 37, Graham had turned his game around and run off four birdies in five holes. He had just

16th
PAR 4
491 YARDS

17th
PAR 4
365 YARDS

Nothing happened; the threat probably was a hoax.

Green hung on through some anxious moments over the next four holes. He scraped out a par at the 15th, opened his lead to two strokes by birdieing the 16th, a par 5 then, got down in two putts from 50 feet at the 17th, then bunkered his approach to the 18th.

Digging his feet into the sand, he told himself, "Don't chunk it."

Then he chunked it and left his ball 20 feet short of the hole. His first putt rolled dead 3½ feet short, but he holed his second. With the bogey 5 he shot even-par 70, and his 278 beat Graham by one stroke.

Two days earlier, Sam Snead had said goodbye to the Open. It had been 40 years since he had played in his first, back in 1937. He had been invited to play again as an observance. Snead was 65. He shot 74-78–152 and missed the cut.

birdied the 16th as Green walked off the 13th green, and now Graham had only one stroke to make up.

After hooking into the woods at the 17th, Graham played a miraculous recovery to eight feet but missed his birdie, then moved on to the 18th.

Just then Green was heading for the 15th tee. Harry Easterly, the USGA's president, Sandy Tatum, a vice president, and Charlie Jones, the police lieutenant, stopped him and explained the threat and the reason for all those policemen.

They gave Green three options. He could withdraw, he could ask for play to be suspended, or he could play on.

He chose to play.

18th
PAR 4
466 YARDS

101st U.S. Open

The 18th hole, par 4 and 466 yards.

Tiger Woods had won 21 PGA Tour events in the past 2½ years, including five major championships.

Two days before David Duval played his first stroke of the 101st United States Open Championship, someone asked him if Tiger Woods' winning the Open, British Open, PGA Championship and Masters in succession would ever rank among the benchmark accomplishments in sport, perhaps even ahead of Joe DiMaggio's 56-game hitting streak of 1941.

Duval raised his eyebrows in mock surprise and said, "I'm not aware it isn't already."

When the laughter died, the thought occurred that Duval could be right. What Woods did over the 10 months spanning the 2000 U.S. Open and the 2001 Masters set a standard that defies understanding. Not only had he won them all, he wrecked his competition both in the U.S. and British Opens, squeaked past Bob May in a tense playoff at the PGA Championship, and slipped past Duval and Phil Mickelson at Augusta National Golf Club when neither man took advantage of his openings over the closing holes.

As a further point, since the formation of the modern Grand Slam, no one else had won more than two in succession. At the same time we must understand that Ben Hogan won three in succession in 1953 because, while the PGA Championship ended before he won the British Open, he played the qualifying rounds of the British Open on the same days as the semifinal and final matches of the PGA.

In a reprise of the 1950s, Tommy Bolt, the old warrior who had won the 1958 Open at Southern Hills, jousted with reporters late Wednesday afternoon, the day before the Open began. He spoke of the field and dismissed everyone but Woods.

"It's down to one," he said.

Warming to the subject, Bolt said, "I know none of you guys are going to bet against Tiger Woods."

Then a woman writer said she had already put her money on the field.

"You did, honey?" Tommy asked, his voice rising. "Well, if you took the field you've got almost an even bet."

When someone reminded Bolt that she had 155 others playing for her, he wasn't impressed. "I can't help it," he went on. "The way he plays golf is unbelievable."

Continuing his eulogy, Tommy raved, "He out-drives them, he out-putts them, he out-thinks them. He's got a better short game. You can't put him anywhere that he can't get up and down. We've already seen that. It's unbelievable how good he is. Unless somebody shoots some good rounds, he's going to be unbeatable."

So much for expert testimony.

Clearly, though, Woods had ruled professional golf almost from the day he joined the PGA Tour late in 1996, in time to play eight tournaments before the season ended. He wasn't quite 21, about a year younger than Jack Nicklaus when he joined the tour late in 1961, but he stunned nearly everyone by winning quickly. In a little more than a month, he beat Davis Love III on the fourth hole of a playoff in the Las Vegas Invitational, and two weeks later he nipped Payne Stewart by one stroke and won the Disney World/Oldsmobile Classic.

The following year he opened his first full season by beating Tom Lehman in the Mercedes Championships playoff. Obviously, he was bettering the best players in the game.

Then, as everyone knows, he shot 270 at Au-

Prologue

gusta and not only broke the record score of 271 but won the Masters by 12 strokes. Nicklaus had set the record 32 years earlier, back in 1965, and won by nine strokes. Clearly, Woods was something special.

Over the next few years he showed just how special. After winning two more tournaments in 1997, he slumped the following year and won only the BellSouth Classic on the U.S. tour, although he won one other full-field event in Europe. Then

Only Vijay Singh had beaten Woods in a major in the last two years.

he snapped back and won the PGA Championship and seven other U.S. tournaments in 1999, and nine in 2000, which was overshadowed by his marvelous run of the U.S. Open, the British Open and the PGA Championship. When he won the 2001 Masters, he had won five of the game's last six most important tournaments, the last four in succession. Vijay Singh had broken his string by winning the 2000 Masters.

Going into the Open, Woods had won two Masters, two PGA Championships, one U.S. Open and one British Open — six professional majors altogether by the age of 25. At that stage he had tied Lee Trevino, and needed just one more to match Arnold Palmer, Sam Snead and Gene Sarazen, two to catch Tom Watson, and three more to equal Gary Player and Ben Hogan.

While his is indeed an extraordinary record, comparing it with some others isn't quite fair. Record-keepers credit Bob Jones and Harry Vardon with seven apiece, but there was neither a Masters nor a PGA Championship in Vardon's day, and the U.S. Open wasn't much of a prize. And, of course, as an amateur, Jones wasn't eligible for the PGA, and it was he who invented the Masters after he had retired from competition. We should remember as well that Hogan played in only one British Open, and the Masters wasn't much of a deal until the early 1950s.

This of course doesn't diminish Woods' accomplishment. By the middle 1950s, the Masters had developed into a decidedly big deal.

His record during 1999 and 2000 is truly astonishing. Only three men have won more tournaments in the U.S. in one year than Woods in 2000 — Byron Nelson won 19 in 1945 (prize money for a tournament in New Jersey didn't meet PGA of America standards, but he won it nonetheless); Ben Hogan won 13 in 1946 and 10 two years later; Sam Snead won 11 in 1950; and Paul Runyan in 1933 won nine.

By winning six in succession in 1999-2000, Woods matched Hogan's record of 1948, but one of Hogan's was a four-ball tournament. Of course Nelson's 1945 streak of 11 in succession hasn't been seriously challenged.

To go further, only Nelson, with 26 victories in 1944-45, and Hogan, with 20 in 1946-47, have better two-year records than Woods' 17 in 1999-2000, although Hogan, in 1947-48, and Snead, in 1949-50 won as many.

At times Woods played surreal golf. Winning the NEC Invitational in 2000, he shot 259 over the rugged Firestone Country Club course in Akron, Ohio. Three times he shot 263, once turned in 265, and shot 266 in three other tournaments.

Twice he shot single rounds of 61, first at the 1999 Byron Nelson Classic, a tournament he didn't win, and then at the NEC Invitational in 2000, which he won by 11 strokes over Justin Leonard. He's had two 62s, and three 63s.

In 4½ years, Woods had turned into an incredible scoring machine, and he had shown no hint he would let up. In the three months leading up to the Open, he had played five PGA Tour events and won four of them — Bay Hill, The Players Championship, the Masters and the Memorial.

Like Nicklaus before him, Woods carries a 15th club. He intimidates, sometimes with overpowering rounds, sometimes with Promethean shots. One stroke behind Ernie Els at the 72nd hole of the 2000 Mercedes Championships, Woods ripped a 3-wood to 15 feet and eagled. Poor Els had to hole a 10-footer for a birdie to tie. Woods beat him in the playoff.

There were others. From a downhill lie at the seventh at Muirfield Village Country Club, he flew a 3-iron 234 yards, setting up an eagle 3.

With an arsenal like that, no matter if someone is ripping the course apart, with Woods around, no lead is safe. Even though he was clearly off his game at Southern Hills, no one felt secure as long as Woods had holes to play.

Nevertheless, as the Open began, a

David Duval challenged at Augusta National.

Phil Mickelson needed to prove he could finish strong.

Prologue

Davis Love III already had one major title.

Runner-up in the 1999 PGA, Sergio Garcia was a rising star.

Ernie Els had two U.S. Open victories.

flock of first-rate players were poised to take a shot.

Off past performances on big occasions, Vijay Singh looked like the best bet. Numerical rankings aside, he might have been the second-best player in the game. He had won the 1998 PGA Championship and the 2000 Masters, and while he hadn't won the Open, he had tied for third at Pinehurst Country Club in 1999 and for eighth place at Pebble Beach Golf Links in 2000. He had his flaws, though. An elegant striker of the ball, he was not the world's best putter. Still, he was having a good year — second at Pebble Beach and in The Players Championship, tied for third three times, tied for fourth at Bay Hill and for fifth place in the Memorial.

Duval and Phil Mickelson had to be considered. They had been perennial challengers, and Duval had made a run at Woods in the British Open the previous July and at Augusta in April. Sitting in second place at St. Andrews, six behind as the last round opened, Duval made up three strokes in seven holes, but when he missed a makeable birdie putt at the 10th, a short par 4 that can be driven, he was finished. Duval made another run at Woods in the Masters, but with birdie chances at five of the last six holes, he made only one and finished second, beaten by two strokes. Still, he had been playing first-class golf leading up to the Open; nine of his last 12 rounds had been in the 60s.

Mickelson had been having a decent year as well, finishing among the top three in eight tournaments, including a third-place finish at the Masters. Like Duval, he could have done better at Augusta National, but he showed a weakness on putts inside four feet, the kind that must be holed if championships are to be won. Nor had he proved himself a strong finisher. In nine previous Opens in which he made the cut, he had never closed with a round in the 60s. Neither had he done much better in the first three — in 38 rounds over 10 Opens, he'd had only four scores in the 60s.

Jesper Parnevik was a major threat.

Lee Westwood led the Europeans.

Then there was Ernie Els. He'd been an enigma almost from the beginning. One of the 19 men who have won at least two Opens, he came to Southern Hills with a spotty record for the year. Although he had tied for sixth in the Masters, in his other 11 appearances he had three third-place finishes and one fourth but nothing higher than 25th place in the others. He began the Memorial with 69, one stroke behind Woods, but finished with two 75s and a 77 and sank to a tie for 63rd place. All that aside, Els could be capable of shooting any kind of score when he was on his game.

There were others worth watching as well: from Europe came 21-year-old Sergio Garcia, whose enthusiasm makes him so appealing; Lee Westwood; Jesper Parnevik, who usually plays well on the big occasions; Thomas Bjorn; Padraig Harrington, who had finished high in both the U.S. and British Opens a year ago; and Colin Montgomerie, still on a fruitless search for a major title.

Among other tour players, Davis Love III already had a major title, Joe Durant had won two tournaments early in the year, Steve Stricker had won the WGC-Accenture Match Play, which opened the 2001 season, and David Toms had surprised his hometown fans by winning at New Orleans.

On the other hand, no one gave a thought to Mark Brooks, Rocco Mediate or Retief Goosen.

Colin Montgomerie was back again.

At 5:30 Thursday morning, an hour before the first group teed off, fans had already packed the grandstand overlooking the first hole, expecting to witness the opening scene of a historic four days.

Over the previous 12 months, Tiger Woods had won the U.S. Open, the British Open, the PGA Championship and the Masters Tournament. According to popular belief, he would win a second straight Open.

That's what they expected. What they saw didn't match their expectations. Instead, Woods began his defense with indifferent golf, and Hale Irwin, who understandably wasn't given much thought, shot 67, the best 18-hole score of a short day.

As it had a year earlier, bad weather shut down the championship in mid-afternoon with more than half the 156-man starting field still on the course. Along the way the gallery learned that a 56-year-old man like Irwin could still play with the kids, at least for a round or two, that Woods was not the automaton scoring machine his fans believed, and they learned how to pronounce the name Retief Goosen. They also learned that golf administrators must deal with weather.

Skies had been overcast throughout the morning, and meteorologists had predicted severe weather and warned that tornadoes could be on the way. Toward mid-afternoon the clouds darkened, the wind picked up strength, and the temperature dropped from 90 to 74 degrees. With the storm about to strike, the USGA suspended play at 3:39 p.m. The 90 men left on the course would return at 7 o'clock the following morning to complete their rounds, while the second round would begin at 9 a.m. It was pretty much the same scene as a year earlier at Pebble Beach Golf Links when fog forced suspensions. Meantime, those who had finished would have a long rest before they returned to Southern Hills.

Luckily for him, Irwin went off at 8 a.m., early enough to finish. Woods, though, played only nine holes and left the course three over par, facing a putt of six feet for a par after bunkering his approach to the 10th.

Loren Roberts had gone out with Irwin and shot 69, along with Stewart Cink, who would be around at the end. Angel Cabrera of Argentina, the first man off the tee at 6:30, shot even-par 70 along with Phil Mickelson, Sergio Garcia and Matt Gogel, a Tulsa native who as an 11-year-old had seen Raymond Floyd win the 1982 PGA Championship at Southern Hills.

Both Mickelson and Davis Love III could have done better. Out in 35, Mickelson had dipped to two under par with birdies at the 10th and 13th, but as he had done so often in the past, he gave them away faster than he had won them. He missed the greens on both the 14th, a par 3, and 15th, a drive-and-pitch par 4.

Bothered by neck and back problems that had kept him out of competition for two months, Love dazzled the gallery with a display of slick scrambling. Even though he missed the greens at five of the first six holes, he still shot 35 going out, and then played worse. On the first seven holes of the second nine he hit only two fairways and two greens and yet parred every one. His loose play caught up with him in the end. Even

Although a three-time U.S. Open champion, Hale Irwin (67) started far above most people's expectations.

First Round

The first man off at 6:30, Angel Cabrera (70) of Argentina posted a score that few would better.

Retief Goosen (66) played 11 holes Friday.

though he hit the last two fairways, he missed each green, bogeyed both, and shot 72. Scrambling at its best.

Perhaps it was done by whim, but by sending Irwin off with Roberts and Fred Funk, the USGA created a grouping whose combined ages totaled 146 years. Neither Irwin nor Roberts played as if they needed special help, although Irwin stumbled at first.

He began by missing both the first two greens and bogeying, but Irwin had been around long enough not to panic. Instead he struck back, holed a 20-footer at the third, then punched a 7-iron about a foot from the hole of the fourth. Back to even par. Another birdie at the eighth, at 225 yards the longest of the par-3 holes, and he turned for home in 34.

Another birdie at the 10th and Irwin was two under par. After he overshot the 12th, he holed from 10 feet to save par, picked up another birdie at the 14th, another par 3, lost the stroke at the 15th, and then ran home a 25-footer to save another par at the 491-yard 16th. When it fell he

101st U.S. Open

Mike Weir (67) saved par from a bunker at the 18th, which ranked as the most difficult hole of the championship.

First Round

Retief Goosen	66	-4
Hale Irwin	67	-3
Mike Weir	67	-3
J.L. Lewis	68	-2
Loren Roberts	69	-1
Stewart Cink	69	-1
Jeff Maggert	69	-1
Chris DiMarco	69	-1
Toshimitsu Izawa	69	-1

pumped his fist, turned to his caddie and mouthed, "Wow!"

But the best was yet to come.

Safely past the 17th, he faced a shot he had played superbly so many times in the past — a 2-iron to a distant green. He had played that shot in his greatest moments — into the 18th at Winged Foot 27 years earlier when he won the first of his three Opens, into the 13th at Inverness in 1979, setting up an eagle 3 and his second Open, and into the 16th at Medinah in 1990 when he won his third.

Now Irwin's drive down the slope of the 18th fairway left him still another 2-iron. He played it just as he had those others. As he ripped into it, the ball bore through the light wind, cleared the deep bunker guarding the front and braked within a foot or so of the hole. An easy birdie. When the putt fell, he twirled his cap above his head, waved to the gallery and walked off.

Flushed with confidence, Irwin made it clear he had come to win.

"My purpose is not to be ceremonial. It's to be competitive, and I think today established bona fide credentials."

But the day wasn't over. As the old man reveled in the moment, out on the course the young man struggled to survive. It was quite a change for Tiger Woods.

Crowds had begun lining the first fairway long before his 12:30 starting time, but there was no sense of the frenzy of a year earlier.

First Round

Tiger Woods (74) had to take a drop and needed to one-putt for his par at the 534-yard 13th hole.

J.L. Lewis (68) was in lofty company.

Nor was there good reason, because Woods was doing nothing to excite anyone. He missed seven fairways, 10 greens and putted far below what we've come to expect. Take the third hole. With the hole set on the right, and his drive pushed into the right rough, he pulled his approach to the left side of the green and left his first putt about 10 feet short. Then he missed, taking a bogey after scrambling for pars at the first two holes.

Another loose approach to the fourth and another putt that pulled up short evidently drained the spirit from him, because as he walked ever so slowly off the fourth green and up the slope to the fifth tee, he wore an expression of either bewilderment or gloom. It's possible he had sensed earlier that all was not well. After he pushed his drive almost into the gallery at the opening hole, wearing what looked like a resigned smile, he stepped away, almost as if he recognized his game wasn't in order. Now he sensed he was in trouble. It grew worse at the ninth.

A long drive up the left side set up a clear shot at the flagstick, set close to the right edge halfway

101st U.S. Open

Stewart Cink (left), Toshimitsu Izawa (center) and Chris DiMarco (right) were among the five with 69s.

Jeff Maggert (69) again was a major contender.

Loren Roberts (69) played well in Irwin's group.

First Round

Hal Sutton (70) wanted to regain his 2000 form.

back. Going for it, Woods hit a high pitch, but as the ball took off, someone called, "Fore right." It drifted toward a tree, nipped a branch, and dropped into a bunker. A bladed recovery from a thin lie flew the ball over the green into a heavy lie. His pitch rolled four feet past the hole, and he missed coming back. He made a double-bogey 6 and was out in 38.

By then everyone knew the storm was about to break. Lightning flashed above the Tulsa skyline, and warning horns blared — just as Woods pitched out of the bunker at the 10th.

Quickly, spectators evacuated the grandstands and boarded buses to parking lots, while a fleet of vans rushed the players to the clubhouse, where they were to wait out the storm. Soon rain gushed down and soaked the course. Within an hour the USGA realized golf was over for the day and everyone left for home.

Except for the grounds crew. By 8 p.m. they were back at work, repairing the damage.

With the last grouping of the second round scheduled to tee off at 5:30 p.m. Friday, everyone realized this would be perhaps the longest day in Open history. Before anyone could think of that,

Sergio Garcia (70) came with aspirations for the title.

Ernie Els scored 71, finishing on Friday.

though, there were still the 90 men who hadn't finished the first round to deal with. When the last putt dropped, at 12:42 Friday afternoon, the first round had finished 30 hours and 12 minutes after it started.

Before the storm swept through, Retief Goosen had played the first seven holes in three under par. Beginning at the eighth Friday morning, he ran off two more quick birdies to go five under. Out in 30, he added another birdie at the vulnerable 13th, and at that stage had moved three strokes ahead of Irwin, resting in his hotel room.

A 32-year-old South African veteran of the PGA European Tour, Goosen had to hole a putt to bogey the long 16th, then lost another when he overshot the 17th and missed a five-foot putt. Four under now, he made a routine par at the 18th, came back in 36, and shot 66.

Toshimitsu Izawa, a Japanese golfer only marginally less well known in the United States than Goosen, had played four holes in two under on Thursday, picked up more strokes Friday morning and stood four under through the 12th, but bogeyed the next three and shot 69.

Up ahead, Woods holed his par putt at the 10th, but he still struggled. He dropped another stroke at the testing 12th, and then won it back by birdieing the 15th, a 412-yard hole where the short yardage was deceptive. It wasn't easy. When Woods' pitch hit, he had ended a string of seven consecutive holes without hitting a green in regulation, an indication of the sloppy golf he had been playing.

He shot a grim 74.

When the first round ended, Goosen held the lead, one stroke ahead of Irwin and the left-handed Canadian Mike Weir, who holed his pitch for an eagle 2 at the 10th. Alone in fourth place sat J.L. Lewis, a 40-year-old club professional from Texas who had dropped off the PGA Tour for three years in the early 1990s and played the Nike Tour in 1997.

Woods, meanwhile, had fallen far behind, tied with 24 others in the unfamiliar territory of 63rd place. He had to wonder if he'd be around Sunday.

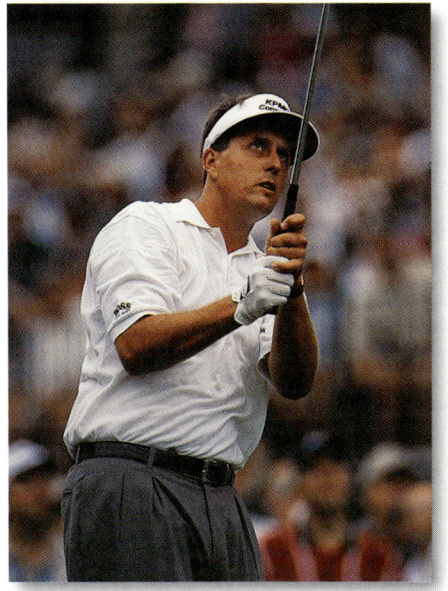
Phil Mickelson (70) made three bogeys.

David Duval (70) had a double bogey.

The weather front passed through overnight and Friday dawned calm and clear except for a few wispy clouds drifting through the morning sky. By midday even they had passed, and the warming sun pushed the temperature into the 80s, but the course showed the effects of an inch and a half of rainfall.

Where drives had scooted miles after hitting the hard ground the day before, now they plopped into softer ground and pulled up quickly. With the course playing slightly longer, the players in general played their approaches with longer clubs but, helping matters, pitches braked quickly on putty-like greens and misdirected drives didn't always run away and bury themselves in the tangled rough.

Rain-soaked fairways had their drawbacks, though. With the ground soft, and in some places soggy, groundskeepers mowed only the greens, leaving the grass to grow slightly shaggy on fairways and tees. As a consequence, irons couldn't be struck quite so crisply.

The wind had shifted overnight as well, most notably changing the nature of the 13th and 16th holes. They could still be reached with strong second shots, but they called for longer clubs. David Duval, for example, swung so hard trying to reach the 13th green with his second shot, he almost fell over backward.

It was worth it. His ball cleared the pond guarding the right side of a narrow causeway, settled just off the green's collar and he birdied, dropping to one under par. Duval shot 69, climbing into a tie for sixth place.

While Duval was moving up, Hale Irwin was dropping down. Irwin had captured the fans' admiration with his wonderful opening 67, but even with a long rest between his finish early Thursday afternoon and his late starting time Friday, he showed that, at 56, he had lost the staying power of his prime years.

This wasn't new; Irwin had shown the effects of aging a year earlier at Pebble Beach. He had opened with 68, three under par once again, but he had nothing more to give, followed with 78 and 81 and dropped from sight.

Now, beginning his second round at 5:15 p.m., he shot 75 and, at 142, fell to a 17th-place tie. Although his fans hoped he would rebound and threaten the leaders once again, few truly believed he could. In the end he closed with 74 and 76 and tied for 52nd place with 292.

Granted that Irwin broke a few hearts, there were other, pleasant surprises. Forty-year-old Mark Brooks, for example, who had fallen off the charts after winning the 1996 PGA Championship, shot to the top of the leaderboard with a round of 64, matching the second-lowest score ever shot in the Open. With 136 at the end of the second round, he stood in a first-place tie alongside Retief Goosen, who added a par round of 70 to his opening 66, and J.L. Lewis, with a second 68.

Young Sergio Garcia romped around Southern Hills with only one bogey, shot 68 and climbed into a tie for fourth at 138 with Stewart Cink, who had played two steady 69s. Duval followed at 139, alongside local hero Matt Gogel, Rocco Mediate and Phil Mickelson, who inspired the loudest cheer of the day by holing an 8-iron for a hole-in-one at the 175-yard sixth. On its first bounce, Mickelson's ball dived into the hole. This was his second

Mark Brooks (136) shot 64 while hitting 12 of 14 fairways and 15 greens.

Second Round

Retief Goosen (136) shot 70, but could have done better.

The surprising J.L. Lewis (136) stayed with the leaders.

miracle of the day; he had chipped in for a birdie at the first hole.

Asked if the hole-in-one had given him hope his time had come, Mickelson grinned and said, "It's a good omen."

Perhaps, but it helped only marginally. Making the same mistakes that have haunted him on other big occasions, Mickelson bogeyed both the 10th and 11th with mis-played approaches, and instead of a truly significant score that would jump him toward the top, he shot 69.

Out on the course, still playing inconsistent golf, Tiger Woods spent most of the round wondering if he would make the 36-hole cut, projected at six-over-par 146. Needing 72, he shot 71 — two strokes to the good. At 145, he became one of the 79 men who survived, one of the largest fields that ever played the Open's last two rounds.

Among others who had placed high after 18 holes, Loren Roberts, like Irwin, had a bad day, shot 76, and fell from fifth to 43rd place; Jeff Maggert went from 69 to 73 and fell to 17th; Toshimitsu Izawa slipped from 69 to 74 and dropped from fifth to 23rd, alongside Mike Weir, who followed his opening 67 with 76.

Finding Brooks at the head of the pack may have been as surprising as seeing Goosen up there with him. A slightly built man at 5-foot-9 and 150 pounds, Brooks had played the PGA Tour since 1984 and had won seven times between 1988 and 1996. He reached the peak of his career by defeating Kenny Perry in a playoff at the PGA.

But Brooks was no longer playing with his old cocky assurance. From the time he won the PGA in 1996, he started in 143 tournaments. He placed in the top 10 only nine times and missed 51 cuts. But he left no question that he played his heart out over the middle three rounds at Southern Hills, beginning with his impeccable 64.

Brooks was among those left on the course by Thursday's storm. Playing just behind Goosen, he stood one over par through the first seven holes. After play resumed Friday morning, he birdied the 165-yard 11th to get back to even par, but with a par round in hand, he double-bogeyed the 18th, a hole that would haunt him later. At 72, he stood

101st U.S. Open

Sergio Garcia (138) shot 68 with one bogey.

Stewart Cink (138) had a pair of 69s.

Although Tiger Woods (145) did not hole this shot for birdie at the 17th, he did shoot 71 and made the cut by one.

Second Round

Matt Gogel (139) had a hometown crowd.

Rocco Mediate (139) pulled close with 68.

six strokes off the lead when the round ended.

With barely 45 minutes to reorganize himself before starting out again, Brooks put a different driver in his bag. Throughout the first round he had struggled to keep the ball in play. He felt his driver wasn't doing the job and put it aside. Immediately he birdied five of the first six holes and was off on the week's finest round, one that equaled the second-round scoring record.

He hit the first nine fairways. He nearly knocked the flagstick from the hole with his 6-iron to the first green, holed his putt from a foot, and followed with a 4-iron to 12 feet at the second and another birdie.

Barely missing another at the third, Brooks ran off three more birdies, pitching to four feet at the fourth, playing an 8-iron third shot to seven feet at the endless fifth and then holing from 30 feet at the 175-yard sixth.

Now five under for the round, he scrambled for his par 3 at the eighth, played a nice recovery from a bunker and saved another at the ninth and made the turn for home in 30. After a routine par at the 10th, he played another 7-iron to the 165-yard 11th and holed from 14 feet for his sixth birdie.

From the 12th through the 17th he missed only the 13th fairway and strung together a series

David Duval (139) was three off the lead.

Phil Mickelson (139) said his ace was "a good omen."

Thomas Bjorn (141) posted a second-round 69.

Angel Cabrera (141) was steady again.

Second Round

Retief Goosen	66 - 70 – 136	-4
Mark Brooks	72 - 64 – 136	-4
J.L. Lewis	68 - 68 – 136	-4
Sergio Garcia	70 - 68 – 138	-2
Stewart Cink	69 - 69 – 138	-2
David Duval	70 - 69 – 139	-1
Phil Mickelson	70 - 69 – 139	-1
Rocco Mediate	71 - 68 – 139	-1
Matt Gogel	70 - 69 – 139	-1
Jim Furyk	70 - 70 – 140	E

either. Brooks carries a bunch with him, some with different heads but a similar shaft, some with a similar head and different shafts, some with different heads and different shafts. Here he changed to a driver with the same head but a different shaft.

Whether it helped or not can't be said for certain, but the results suggest he was right. Where he had hit only eight of 14 fairways in the first round, he hit 12 in the second. He played better approaches as well, and he putted a little better. He hit 15 greens and one-putted nine holes in the second round, where he had hit 11 greens, one-putted eight and three-putted another in the first.

of two-putt pars. Then he missed the 18th fairway and bunkered his approach. After pitching out with what he described as "a very acceptable bunker shot," he holed still another putt from 12 feet and came back in 34.

Pressed about whether he had been aware of the Open scoring record of 63, Brooks seemed annoyed.

"It's not that big a deal," Brooks claimed. "I'm not interested in one-round numbers. It's like my putt on 18. Was I trying to make it? Yes. Did I care if I made it? I was trying to make sure I didn't three-putt, to be honest with you. The thing wiggled about eight different directions, and it just fell in. I was lucky."

Apparently, switching drivers wasn't a big deal

Jim Furyk (140) double-bogeyed the 17th.

Second Round

Paul Azinger (141) recovered with 67.

Davis Love III (141) came in with 69.

Kirk Triplett (141) had a second-day 69.

While Brooks was playing his record-matching round, Goosen was playing the steadiest golf imaginable. He had run off 12 consecutive pars before birdieing the 13th and moved ahead of Brooks, playing one hole behind him. Goosen fell back by missing the green of the 14th, a 215-yard par 3, moved ahead again with another birdie at the 17th, but fell back again by missing an eight-footer for a par at the 18th. He had shot 35-35, an even-par round but one where he might have scored lower.

Playing textbook golf, Goosen had missed only the 12th fairway, and for the second consecutive round he hit 14 greens. But he didn't take advantage of it. Anyone who strikes the ball this well might expect to birdie more than two holes.

Watching him play such first-class golf through two rounds led to the question of why he hadn't done better on the PGA European Tour, where he plays most of his golf. He had a candid answer:

"I haven't played well enough," Goosen admitted. "The game goes funny sometimes. Sometimes you're playing really well but not scoring. That's the way I've played the last four tournaments. I felt like I was hitting the ball quite well but wasn't scoring.

"Last week I found something in my putting and started doing quite a little bit better. I feel maybe I can do something this week."

As we might expect, Woods felt just about the same. When Brooks finished, he pointed out that if he could shoot 64, it certainly wasn't beyond Tiger Woods.

At one stage, as he swung into the second nine, Woods looked as if he might have found his usual game. Out in 37 with bogeys at the fourth and fifth, he played two stunning shots into the 12th and 13th, a pair of perfectly gauged pitches to holes cut on the front of the greens and tucked behind bunkers. Not taking the dare, Woods aimed right of the bunkers, dropped his ball just beyond the collars and holed both putts.

Watching those two exquisite shots, the gallery felt a surge of excitement, and raced after him to the 14th, greedy for more. But Woods had no more birdies in him. He dropped another stroke at the 16th and finished with 71.

When the round ended, he stood nine strokes behind Goosen, Brooks and Lewis, but he had come from behind in the past. Not in the Open, though. Still hoping, he pointed to Brooks' 64 and said, "You play a good, solid round and you're going to move up."

Hale Irwin (75) couldn't keep the pace.

When Goosen and Brooks finished, the sun still shone brightly, but it was 4:15 in the afternoon and the 111 players left on the course still had many holes to play. All but 33 finished, some in semi-darkness.

With the clock about to strike 9 o'clock, Cink holed a short putt to par the 18th and finished with his second 69, and minutes later Steve Jones, the 1996 Open champion, bogeyed the 18th. At six over par, he survived for the last two rounds.

The cut eliminated a number of prominent players. Nick Price was among them.

Seven years earlier Price had stood at the top of the game. He had won the PGA Championship in 1992, and reached his peak two years later. In July 1994 he won the British Open, holing a monstrous putt across the 17th green at Turnberry, and a month later he burned the grass off Southern Hills by shooting 67-65-70-67–269 and winning the PGA once again. Not in 70 years had one man held both the British Open and the PGA Championship in the same year. Walter Hagen had held them in 1924.

Price was the best player in the game then, but he was 44 now, and as it does with all the old champions, age had claimed its dues. In his Southern Hills encore, Price shot a pair of 74s and, with 148, missed the cut.

Two weeks older than Price, Mark O'Meara missed the cut with 148 as well. Three years earlier O'Meara had won both the Masters and British Open.

Jose Maria Olazabal, the 1999 Masters champion, shot 149; Paul Lawrie, the 1999 British Open champion, and Miguel Angel Jimenez, second to Woods in 2000, shot 150; and Lee Westwood and Justin Leonard, the 1997 British Open champion, shot 151.

With his mother and father walking in his gallery, Gary Nicklaus shot 152. Jack Nicklaus hadn't been outside the ropes at an Open since he was a teenager.

On a happier note, Thongchai Jaidee, a 31-year-old former paratrooper in the Thailand army,

Thongchai Jaidee (146) stayed.

Nick Price (148) departed.

shot 146 and lived to play the full 72 holes of his first Open. A determined man, he had gone through both the local and sectional qualifying rounds just to get to Southern Hills. He had come to the U.S. a year earlier and tried to play at Pebble Beach but missed qualifying.

Perseverance paid off. Now he had made good where others with glossier credentials hadn't.

Retief Goosen (205) had some remarkable recoveries to shoot 69 while hitting six fairways and nine greens.

101st U.S. OPEN
Third Round

When he arrived at Southern Hills, Retief Goosen brought along a reputation as a superior ball-striker but an indifferent putter. Obviously somebody wasn't paying attention. In three rounds over greens with more humps than a cheap mattress, Goosen had holed nearly every putt he had looked at, played 54 holes in five under par, and held at least a share of first place in every round. His 69 in the third round tied him with Stewart Cink.

With 205, they stood one stroke ahead of Mark Brooks, who hadn't been this high on the leaderboard this late in years, the irrepressible young Spaniard Sergio Garcia and Rocco Mediate, who had never placed higher than 25th in seven Opens — five men within one stroke of the lead.

Beginning at one-under 139, Phil Mickelson had played some first-class golf, battled to four under par, but even though he lost a stroke over the last nine holes, he shot 68, and at 207 moved within two strokes of first place and three ahead of Paul Azinger, a bit of a surprise, and David Duval, who had shown no spark at all.

With the exuberance of youth, Garcia was having fun. Thinking back to Pebble Beach, where Tiger Woods ran away with the Open, he looked at the tightly packed leaderboard and quipped, "Well, it isn't going to be won by 12 strokes."

This was another long day. The players who hadn't finished their second rounds came back at 7 a.m. to complete their last few holes, and then the field had to be re-paired. As a result, the third round started late and ended well past 8 p.m. But finally the Open was back on schedule.

While it may have run late, the day was filled with spectacular golf. Cink, a tall, powerful Alabaman, brushed aside a dreadful start and shot 67, along with Mediate, one of the men who showed up at 7 a.m. After turning in 33 on the home nine, Mediate waited hours before starting out on the third round.

Altogether, 16 men shot in the 60s. They did it over a course that had become more difficult each day. The sun burned down and the wind came up, drying the ground and turning the greens hard and fast.

When the USGA announced the 16th would be converted from a par-5 hole, as it had been in previous big events, to a 491-yard par 4, everyone cringed, suspecting a hole this long would be unreasonable. It wasn't. Shortly before noon of the first day, Scott Johnson, a 27-year-old Texan, pounded his drive 335 yards, leaving himself 156 yards to the green, nothing more than an 8- or 9-iron for his approach. This was not Gulliver in a land of Lilliputians. Johnson stands 5-foot-8 and weighs 165 pounds.

Think of the distance the top players hit their iron clubs. Playing the 175-yard sixth hole, Goosen reached the green with a 9-iron. Two holes later, playing into the wind, he ripped a 3-iron onto the eighth green, a shot of 225 yards. Mickelson is even longer, and, of course, so is Woods. The stronger players could reach the fifth with their second shots, even though it stretched 642 yards. Garcia went for it with an iron. He missed, but only because he hit a poor shot.

Meantime, as Garcia, Mickelson, amateur Bryce Molder, Mike Weir and Corey Pavin were shooting 68s, Southern Hills had caught up with J.L. Lewis, who had surprised everyone by playing so well through the first two rounds. Begin-

Third Round

Stewart Cink (205) was three over after two holes.

Third Round

Stewart Cink	69 - 69 - 67 – 205	-5
Retief Goosen	66 - 70 - 69 – 205	-5
Rocco Mediate	71 - 68 - 67 – 206	-4
Sergio Garcia	70 - 68 - 68 – 206	-4
Mark Brooks	72 - 64 - 70 – 206	-4
Phil Mickelson	70 - 69 - 68 – 207	-3
Paul Azinger	74 - 67 - 69 – 210	E
David Duval	70 - 69 - 71 – 210	E
Mike Weir	67 - 76 - 68 – 211	+1
Jim Furyk	70 - 70 - 71 – 211	+1

ning the day tied with Goosen and Brooks, he began falling apart when he bogeyed the fifth. Out in 37, he came back in 40 and dropped eight strokes behind the leaders at 213.

Even so, he was still one stroke ahead of Woods, who finally shot a round under par. With his enthusiastic gallery cheering every good shot and moaning over the not so good, Woods shot 69, along with seven others. Starving for birdies, Woods made four this day, more than in the first two rounds combined. He wasted three of them, though, and left the grounds nine strokes out of first, back in 23rd place at 214, tied with six others, including the amateur Molder. Still, his first sub-par round raised hopes he might do something special in the last round.

"I'm in a tough spot," he admitted, then went on, "but you know what? If I play a good solid round tomorrow, you never know."

No matter what he might shoot, he'd still have to pass 22 others, principally the resilient Goosen, whose astonishing ability to recover from impossible positions upset the scouting report. How he held onto first place is difficult to explain, as he hit only six fairways and nine greens and yet shot 69.

Cink's game wasn't much sharper. He hit only eight fairways and 10 greens, but after dropping three strokes at the first two holes, he played the remaining 16 holes in six under par and climbed from a tie for fourth to a tie for first. He was the only man in the field to have played all three rounds in the 60s.

Festive marquees provided hospitality facilities.

Woods had teed off hours before Goosen and Brooks, who brought up the rear. He had hoped to birdie a few of the early holes and perhaps put a scare into the field, but he put himself in trouble at the first hole and couldn't make anything happen. Adding to his troubles, he bogeyed the ninth again, once more hitting the same tree that had cost him a double-bogey 6. His ball tumbled into the same bunker, and after blading his recovery over the green, he holed an eight-footer to save a bogey.

Altogether, this had been a frustrating round for the defending champion. Putts that seemed to jump into holes in past tournaments grazed the edges and glided past. One caught the lip, looked in, but spun away. Woods was looking at formidable odds if he hoped to catch up.

Certainly Cink had been playing well recently

Rocco Mediate (206) credited his short game.

Third Round

Mark Brooks (206), who two-putted for a par here at the 12th, liked his position after 54 holes.

Sergio Garcia (206) posted a second straight 68.

and shown no signs of weakness. He had tied for eighth in the Open at Pebble Beach a year ago, and even though Woods beat him by eight strokes at the Memorial Tournament two weeks before he came to Southern Hills, he had placed fourth, ahead of most of the men he faced here.

If his fumbling start had upset him, it didn't show. In three rounds he hadn't parred the first hole yet, but he had started the day two strokes out of first place and now he found himself five strokes behind.

Quickly, though, he holed a nice putt for a birdie at the fourth, added another at the long fifth, played an 8-iron to three feet and birdied the sixth, and from 153 yards pitched within holing distance and ran in still another birdie putt at the seventh — four in succession.

One under through the first nine, he headed for friendly ground. Cink had played the second nine in 31 in the opening round, and while he didn't match it in the third, his 33 wasn't bad. He made a two-putt birdie at the 13th and holed another putt at the 412-yard 15th. He was five under par and the Open title was within reach.

Out on the course, Mickelson celebrated his 31st

birthday with a barrage of birdies. Beginning the day at 139, one under par and three behind Goosen and Brooks, he birdied the first, reaching two under, and after backing off three times, holed from inside six feet and birdied the third.

Mickelson had played some classic irons, and his putting had been of another world. His perfectly gauged pitch to the fourth just cleared a bunker on the left front, and when a curling 25-probable eagle 3, Mickelson three-putted. With two more birdies offset by two bogeys, he closed with 36, but with 68 he had gained ground.

Brooks, meanwhile, had bogeyed the fifth. Three under now, he had fallen two strokes behind Goosen. From there on he parred every hole until finally a putt dropped at the 15th. Back to four under, still a stroke behind both Cink and Goosen, both of them five under by then.

Phil Mickelson (207) was pleased despite three bogeys.

Paul Azinger (210) had fought back to even par.

footer dropped at the fifth, he had one-putted four of the first five holes. Out in 32 after saving pars at the seventh and eighth, Mickelson had played 27 holes with just 36 putts.

Precision golf like this is nearly impossible to keep up. His approach to the 10th plugged in a bunker, costing him one stroke, and three holes later he squandered a superb 225-yard iron shot into the 13th that settled no more than 10 feet behind the hole. Looking at a certain birdie and

Goosen was playing strange golf, placing himself in impossible positions, then playing impossible recoveries, all the while behaving as if his loose shots amused him. When he played a terrible drive at the ninth — the ball screamed away on a low line into the left rough, looking as if he had nearly whiffed it — he strolled away munching on a section of orange. His attitude seemed as casual as his legato swing.

Once to the ball, he turned what had begun as

Third Round

Tiger Woods (214) bogeyed the ninth hole after taking a double bogey there in the first round.

David Duval (210) was tied for seventh after three days.

a troubling hole into a triumph. While a playful squirrel romped through the grass nearby, Goosen quit smiling long enough to punch a shot that squirted onto the green and dribbled within 10 feet for a birdie. He was five under now.

Goosen's second nine is difficult to believe. He hit only three greens and yet parred every hole. Some samples:

After his tee shot missed the 11th green and ran down a sharp slope, he putted his ball up the hill close enough for an easy par.

In the same position after overshooting the 12th, he putted once again and saved another.

Bunkered at the 14th, another par 3, he pitched to 15 feet and holed again.

A 6-iron left of the 15th green, a lob to five feet, and he holed still another.

A drive into a bunker at the 16th, an iron into another bunker with his second, a pitch and one more good putt.

This string of successive marvels had left the gallery gasping. But more were coming.

The drama reached its peak at the two closing

101st U.S. Open

Mike Weir (211) shot 68.

Duffy Waldorf (212) had 69.

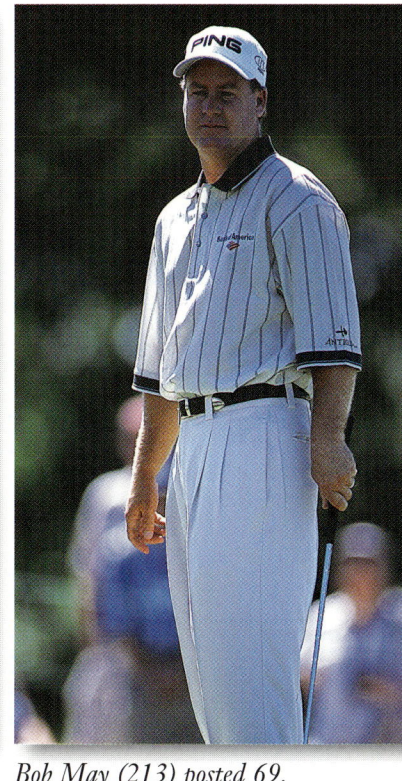

Bob May (213) posted 69.

Jim Furyk (211) shared ninth place.

Corey Pavin (213) shot 68 to move from 43rd to 16th.

Third Round

Tom Lehman (213) had 69 to advance.

Amateur Bryce Molder (214) came in with 68.

Loren Roberts (214) had shot 69, 76 and 69 again.

Large crowds attended Southern Hills for the club's third U.S. Open Championship, following 1958 and 1977.

holes. His ball lying in shaggy grass over the 17th green, maybe 35 or 40 feet from the hole, Goosen laid back the face of his wedge and took a full swing. The ball popped up, carried onto the green, rolled toward the hole and for a heart-stopping moment looked as if it would fall. Instead, it barely slipped past the edge and stopped two or three inches from the lip. Goosen's caddie hung his head, and when he looked up again, he was laughing. Goosen's smile grew just a little.

Another drive got away from him at the 18th and settled in the right rough. With the green partially blocked by low-hanging branches, Goosen played one of the memorable shots of recent Opens. As he whipped into a 3-iron, the ball darted under the trees, shot into the face of the upslope, barely missed the left greenside bunker, then drifted to the back of the green, hole high.

The gallery roared, and once again Goosen broke into that almost-smile. It was indeed a wonderful shot. His putt ran a few feet past and, of course, he holed it coming back.

He was five under, tied for first. A player whose name very few had recognized three days earlier headed into the fourth round in prime position to win the game's most important championship.

101st U.S. OPEN
Fourth Round

By 1:15 Sunday afternoon the greatest winning streak in major championships since the days of Bob Jones ended when Tiger Woods bogeyed the second hole at Southern Hills. He would not win his second consecutive U.S. Open and fifth straight major championship.

Shortly after 7 p.m., no one was talking about the streak. By then the gallery had been left wondering if there had ever been a day like this in all of championship golf. Three accomplished professionals had come to the 18th hole tied at five under par and not one of them could par the hole. Had any one of them scored a 4, he would have won.

Instead, all three blundered, setting up an 18-hole playoff the next day, the first since 1994.

Mark Brooks botched it first. On the green with two solid shots, he left his second putt dangling over the edge of the hole and bogeyed.

Retief Goosen and Stewart Cink came along two groups later. Cink pulled his approach into the rough, pitched to about 15 feet, three-putted as well, then stepped aside to let Goosen win the Open.

After a stunning approach, Goosen's ball lay no more than 12 feet from a birdie. Considering how he had putted throughout the week, he was a good bet to hole it. Even if he missed, he would certainly par, and the championship would be over.

But he didn't. He ran his ball two feet past the hole, misjudged the break and missed again; then had to hole an even longer putt for his bogey 5. When the putt dropped, he and Brooks had tied at 276, four under par. With his 6, and 277, Cink headed home.

When Goosen's second putt slid past the hole, the gallery gasped. Back in the clubhouse, where he had been clearing out his locker, even Brooks sympathized. "Golf is a very cruel game at times," he said, "I feel bad for him."

Paul Azinger called it, "the saddest thing I've ever seen in watching sports," and even though he felt badly about his own fumbling finish, Rocco Mediate said, "I was sick to my stomach to see both Cink and Goosen do that. It's almost not fair since they played better than anyone else."

Still unflappable, Goosen admitted he wasn't happy about what he had done, but he added, "What can I do? I'm not going to jump out my hotel window. It's golf, you know."

Following Scarlett O'Hara's script, he concluded with, "Tomorrow is another day."

The anguish aside, it has to be understood that this was not the first time a competent golfer holding the Open in his hands had bungled the finishing hole.

- Facing an 18-foot putt to win the 1946 Open, Ben Hogan three-putted, missing his second from two feet. Had he two-putted, he would have joined Lloyd Mangrum, the ultimate winner, Byron Nelson and Vic Ghezzi in a playoff.
- One year later, Sam Snead missed from 2½ feet at the last hole and lost a playoff to Lew Worsham.
- Bob Rosburg jabbed at a three-footer in 1969 and missed a putt that might have put too much pressure on Orville Moody, an uncertain putter, who came to the final hole with two putts to win. Moody got down in two.

Yet those failures involved single players. No one could remember a time when three men failed so badly.

The gallery was stunned when Retief Goosen (276) failed to hole a putt from two feet to win the championship.

Fourth Round

Mark Brooks (276) had birdies at the 11th and 13th, along with this crucial par save at the 12th hole.

Fourth Round

Mark Brooks	72 - 64 - 70 - 70 – 276	-4
Retief Goosen	66 - 70 - 69 - 71 – 276	-4
Stewart Cink	69 - 69 - 67 - 72 – 277	-3
Rocco Mediate	71 - 68 - 67 - 72 – 278	-2
Tom Kite	73 - 72 - 72 - 64 – 281	+1
Paul Azinger	74 - 67 - 69 - 71 – 281	+1
Vijay Singh	74 - 70 - 74 - 64 – 282	+2
Angel Cabrera	70 - 71 - 72 - 69 – 282	+2
Davis Love III	72 - 69 - 71 - 70 – 282	+2
Kirk Triplett	72 - 69 - 71 - 70 – 282	+2
Phil Mickelson	70 - 69 - 68 - 75 – 282	+2

That all three blundered was a shame, because each man had played sound golf throughout a tense day. None of the leaders had opened a comfortable lead for more than two holes. Midway through the first nine Goosen had moved two strokes ahead of Cink and three ahead of Brooks. By the time he stepped onto the 10th tee, he had dropped back to four under par. Brooks had birdied the 11th, and now he, Goosen and Cink had the championship to themselves.

Sunday had turned into a trying day. Whatever the reason — either the course had dried further, the greens become firmer and faster or because of the intense pressure of a tightly contested championship — Southern Hills was giving up fewer sub-par rounds than on any other day of the Open. Where 19 men had broken par in the second round and 16 in the third, only seven shot in the 60s in the fourth.

At the same time, it could be beaten. Both 51-year-old Tom Kite and workaholic Vijay Singh shot 64s, matching the lowest score Southern Hills ever surrendered under U.S. Open conditions.

They beat the day's next lowest score by four strokes. Jesper Parnevik, who hadn't scored lower than 73, shot 68 and jumped 39 places, from a tie for 69th.

Woods shot his second consecutive 69 and climbed from a tie for 23rd into a tie for 12th at 283. Argentine Angel Cabrera, Scott Hoch and Chris Perry shot the other 69s, but only Cabrera placed among the top 10 scorers. He tied five others for seventh place at 282.

Kite's 64 jumped him to a tie for fifth place at 281, with Azinger, one over par. One stroke out of first place through 54 holes, Mediate fell behind by bogeying the sixth and couldn't catch up. He closed with 72.

On a day that opened with so much hope, but at the same time playing under the tension of high

Rocco Mediate's (278) iron play could not compensate for his erratic putting.

Fourth Round

Paul Azinger (281) was saddened.

Tom Kite (281) shot 64 and rose to a fifth-place tie.

Tiger Woods (283) tied for 12th.

expectations, both Phil Mickelson and Sergio Garcia fell apart. One stroke behind Cink and Goosen at the beginning of the day, Garcia hit 11 greens, as many as he had in the third round, when he shot 68, but he played some dreadfully wild shots and couldn't hole a sizable putt. He finished his week with 77, and dropped into the 12th place tie with Woods and two others.

Mickelson played only moderately better, shot 75, and with 282 tied for seventh.

The tension had been building throughout the morning as once again galleries waited for Woods, hoping for a special kind of round. If he were to win another Open, he would have to strike early and throw a scare into the men so far ahead. Granted he trailed by nine strokes, but Arnold Palmer had made up seven strokes in the last round when he won the 1960 Open and Johnny Miller had made up six when he won in 1973.

Palmer had gone out in 30 at Cherry Hills and Miller had set the Open record by shooting 63 at Oakmont. Woods would need something just as good. By the second hole it had become clear he didn't have it in him.

Pushing his drive among the giant oak and elm trees

101st U.S. Open

The crowd gathering at the 18th green could not have imagined what was in store at the finish.

Phil Michelson (282) shot 75 and tied for seventh place with four others.

Vijay Singh (282) shot 64.

Fourth Round

Angel Cabrera (282) finally broke par.

lining the second fairway, Woods took the chance he could thread his ball through a small opening and maybe reach that distant green. With so much at stake, the gamble was worth the risk. It didn't work. The ball clattered among the trees and Woods bogeyed. He couldn't afford bogeys. The great streak had ended.

As it is with all the great champions, there is no giving up in him. He played his heart out on every shot, battled the course and his own off-color game and shot 69. From a tie for 63rd place after the first round, through determination and strength of will, he had fought his way back within a stroke of the top 10.

It was another hot day. Warmed by a blazing sun, the temperature climbed into the 90s, driving spectators to cluster under arching shade trees. The air was light, without cloying humidity, and the sky was clear with only scattered clouds.

Woods had teed off at 12:45, two hours before Cink and Goosen. Brooks and Mickelson went off together at 2:25, just ahead of Garcia and Mediate. Cink and Goosen played last.

Davis Love III (282) finished with 70.

Kirk Triplett (282) shot 70 to tie for seventh.

Stewart Cink (277) took three putts from 15 feet to double bogey the 18th and fall to third place …

Brooks had been playing methodical golf all week. After a lapse in the first round, he had hit 23 of the 28 fairways on driving holes over the second and third rounds — he hit only eight in the first — but, more important, he had hit 38 of 54 greens, and he had putted nearly as well. In 54 holes, he three-putted only the fifth hole in the first round.

He played steadily through the first four holes, but he missed a putt from 10 feet, bogeyed the fifth and dropped to three under par, two behind Goosen and Cink. Four more steady pars and he reached the turn in 36.

Mediate, meanwhile, had been playing erratic golf. A birdie at the first jumped him into a tie for the lead, but two holes later he bogeyed. Back and forth it went, a birdie then a bogey. When he finished the first nine, he had parred only three holes and still turned in even par.

Nothing went right for him on the homeward nine, though, and Mediate gradually yielded, leaving the Open to Goosen, Cink and Brooks.

Goosen had moved ahead almost from the start, pulling off a miracle save from a drive deep in the woods at the second and rolling up pars while his closest challengers lost strokes. When he holed a putt of about 50 feet from one side of the green to the other and birdied the sixth after Cink had bogeyed the fifth, Goosen had moved two strokes ahead, six under par, with Cink and Mediate four under and Brooks three under.

… just one stroke out of the playoff.

Fourth Round

From 30 feet at the 18th, Brooks hit 12 feet past.

His lead didn't last. Goosen lost strokes at both the eighth and ninth and fell into a tie with Cink and Brooks, who had just birdied the 11th. Mediate had begun dropping strokes by then.

On and on they went, Goosen picking up a stroke with another solid birdie putt at the 10th, then Brooks birdieing both the 11th and 13th holes and dropping to five under. Once again the three men were tied, and now the holes were running out.

Cink broke at the 13th. He pulled his drive into a narrow creek, took a penalty stroke, and bogeyed. One hole later Goosen had his first three-putt green and dropped a stroke at the 14th. Quickly, though, Goosen ran in a delicate putt from the back of the 15th. He was back to five under, tied with Brooks.

Playing two holes ahead, Brooks had reached the dangerous 18th. Two solid shots put him on the green, but from 30 feet or more, he ran his

Goosen had an uphill putt of inside 12 feet on his first try at the 18th, but hit two feet beyond the hole.

putt at least 12 feet past the hole, then misjudged the break on the second putt. It was only his second three-putt green of the week. He walked off convinced he had lost the Open.

About then, Cink lofted a gorgeous wedge and laid it no more than two feet from the hole at the 17th, and he and Goosen moved to the 18th tee tied at five under par. They would seemingly settle the Open between them.

Up first, Cink drove up the left side. From there he had a clear shot at the hole, but he would play his approach from a risky sidehill-downhill lie.

Goosen was in better position. He had played a heady drive, down the right to a level patch of ground at the base of the downslope. From there he was looking at a 170-yard uphill shot to a hole tucked behind a gaping bunker.

Still playing first, Cink yanked his 5-iron. The ball soared left and burrowed into shaggy grass behind and left of the green. He would have a struggle to save par.

Now Goosen. Showing his confidence in his swing, he drew back his 6-iron and played a daring shot directly at the flagstick. He had judged the distance just right. The ball cleared the bunkers, dug into the shallow target and braked no more than 12 feet to the right of the hole. He would have an uphill putt at a birdie.

It is difficult to think of the happenings at the 18th as tragic, since this was, after all, a golf tournament. But it is entirely safe to say it will be remembered along with Sam Snead's horrible 8 at the last hole of the Philadelphia Country Club in the 1939 Open, with Greg Norman's collapse in the 1996 Masters and probably longer than Lee Trevino's third shot at the fifth at St. Andrews in the 1970 British Open, a shot that flew directly at the flagstick and settled next to the hole. On the 13th green. He had aimed at the wrong flag.

Goosen misjudged the break and missed his second putt from two feet, then had a longer putt for his bogey.

Retief Goosen led by five strokes after 10 holes of the playoff and shot 70 to win the championship by two.

As a teenager playing golf in Pietersburg, South Africa, about 20 miles from Johannesburg, Retief Goosen was struck by lightning. A storm had passed, but when he and a friend walked past a copse of trees, a bolt of lightning struck.

"It hit the tree and me," Goosen explained. "When I woke up I was lying in a hospital not knowing what was going on. One moment you're there, the next you're not. I was one of the lucky ones who survive it."

Knowing this, why would anyone believe that because of something like a missed putt, he would show up for a golf match so shaken he wouldn't remember which end of the club to hold, even if he would be playing for the U.S. Open Championship? When he arrived back at Southern Hills Monday morning, as outwardly unconcerned as ever over his date with Mark Brooks, he told anyone who asked that he had gone to bed around 10 p.m. without watching replays of Sunday's finish and slept at least nine hours.

He did admit, though, that he felt as if he needed to win Monday because of what had happened Sunday.

Brooks, on the other hand, felt lucky to be there.

Thinking back to that moment when Goosen let the Open slip away, he said, "He hit two great shots on 18 yesterday and should have won. It was just one of those days."

Comparing the two men, there were similarities and there were contrasts. Both dress pretty much the same: they're bland — pale trousers, pale shirts — and neither man projects much crowd appeal.

The differences between them are more striking. At 5-foot-11 and 180 pounds, Goosen is two inches taller and 30 pounds heavier than Brooks, although he looks even bigger. Goosen has a lazy, unforced swing, while Brooks on the other hand, perhaps because of his size, throws more of himself into his shots. Goosen has thick wrists and powerful forearms, while Brooks' arms, in contrast, look almost delicate.

They play the game differently as well. Brooks relies on hitting fairways and greens, while Goosen, a marvelous iron player who is not one of the game's great drivers, seems likely to recover from anywhere. Apparently he would not survive at this level if he couldn't. Goosen opened the playoff by missing the first three greens and yet played them in even par.

It was this knack, especially his deadly putting, that won the championship for Goosen. He beat Brooks by two strokes, playing Southern Hills in even-par 70.

Actually, the playoff was far from an exhibit of precision golf. Spraying shots all over the lot, Brooks hit only seven fairways all day and Goosen wasn't much better. He hit eight.

Over the Open's regulation 72 holes, Brooks had hit more greens than anyone in the field, and yet on this day, when it mattered so much, he hit only seven. Again, Goosen hit just one more, but where Brooks bogeyed four holes and birdied only two, Goosen birdied three. While Goosen bogeyed three as well, he didn't lose his first stroke until the 12th hole, after he had five shots in hand, and his others at the last two holes when, in effect, the championship was all over.

Over the course of the round, Goosen parred

Playoff

Mark Brooks began to struggle to control his shots, falling further behind.

six holes from off the green, a couple of them in the range of the spectacular. He nearly holed a bunker shot at the first and somehow scraped out a par at the second after his worst drive of the day.

From the first few holes of the playoff, it had become clear that Goosen's command of the delicate short game mattered more than his greater strength. Goosen had played an iron from the first tee while Brooks, playing a 3-wood, out-drove him by 30 yards, and when Goosen's approach dropped into the greenside bunker, Brooks looked as if he might jump ahead at the start.

Actually, he nearly fell behind from the start. Goosen's bunker shot lipped the hole; Brooks was lucky it didn't drop.

Goosen had more magic left. At the second hole, with his drive almost in the parallel seventh fairway, he punched his ball back into play, lofted an 8-iron to eight feet and, why ask, holed the putt. Next he bunkered his approach to the third, and from a plugged lie in the sand, pitched to six feet and once again saved par.

But while Goosen was performing his third miracle, Brooks was taking the lead. He played a neat 9-iron to four feet and birdied. One ahead, but lots of holes to play.

Both men parred the next two holes, but then Goosen caught up by birdieing the sixth, the first of the par 3s, with an 8-iron to six feet, then moved ahead at the seventh when Brooks drove into the rough, took two more strokes to reach the green and bogeyed.

Still plenty of holes were left, but then the playoff turned around. The ninth seems a mild enough par 4, only 374 yards, but it had been troublesome throughout the Open. Tiger Woods never could play it, Phil Mickelson had bogeyed it twice, Sergio Garcia had double-bogeyed in the fourth round and Goosen had bogeyed it in the last round as well. Brooks, though, had made his 4 every day.

By then, though, Brooks had begun losing control of his shots. Here he pulled his drive so close to a towering old elm tree he had barely enough room to draw back his club. With such a restricted backswing he could only scoot his ball a few yards forward, then pitch to the green. Another bad drive had cost him another bogey.

Goosen, meanwhile, pitched to 20 feet and holed a putt that must have taken a two-foot break, and birdied again for a two-stroke swing. Suddenly Goosen led by three strokes with an outgoing 33, two under par.

Now there was another two-stroke swing at the 10th, where Goosen played a stunning pitch from the rough to a front hole position and birdied from 15 feet, while Brooks, in the rough once again, had to lay up and bogeyed. Ahead by five now, Goosen had put the Open out of reach.

Brooks cut two strokes from Goosen's lead by birdieing the 17th as Goosen bogeyed, but when Brooks' 4-wood to the 18th dived into a bunker, only a reprise of Sunday's finish could save him.

Goosen did indeed struggle a bit, playing so

timid an approach his ball reached only the front edge of the green, then tumbled 30 yards back down the hill, but a cautious putt back up to the green and two putts from 20 feet put it away. Brooks saved a 4 and picked up one more stroke, but it didn't matter.

Goosen had won by two strokes and become the fifth foreigner and third South African U.S. Open champion since the end of the Second World War. He followed Gary Player (1965), Tony Jacklin (1970), David Graham (1981) and Ernie Els (1994 and 1997). Like Goosen, Player and Els are South African; Jacklin is English and Graham Australian.

Goosen had played a remarkable, scrambling round. Missing fairways and greens, he had still shot even par over a testing course under severe conditions. His short game had been breathtaking. Five times he missed greens on the first nine and yet made his figures. Seven times he one-putted, only twice for birdies. It was enough to break anyone's spirit.

Later, when the emotions had calmed and the events of the day had begun to fade, Goosen spoke of those moments when he stared at his final five-foot putt. As he stood over the ball, looking as calm and unconcerned as ever, it was only a front.

"My heart was jumping when I played those last two holes," he admitted. "But you've got to trust yourself and do it. I'm not going to stand here and tell you I wasn't shaky.

"It's been a long week," he went on. "It seems like a year. When I holed that last putt, that was quite a relief after what happened yesterday. I wasn't going to let it happen again. I kept my nerves together."

And what about holding the U.S. Open Championship?

"It's a great feeling. What can I say? It's amazing." As soon as he had settled down, he thought about what may lie ahead. He had played the PGA European Tour since 1992 and done reasonably well, although he had not been a big winner. He had won four tournaments, three in France, and had won six others in his native South Africa.

His winning the Open playoff fits a pattern, because Goosen had always been at his best in head-to-head competitions. Representing South Africa in the old Alfred Dunhill Cup, which for years had been played at St. Andrews, he had won 10 consecutive matches. He had also given Woods a battle in the Dunhill, taking him to the last green before yielding.

Goosen became the third South African champion.

At the same time, he has had a dismal record on the big occasions. He had his best U.S. Open finish at Pebble Beach, where he tied for 12th with Paul Azinger, Jose Maria Olazabal and New Zealander Michael Campbell, and twice he tied for 10th in the British Open, most recently over brutally hard Carnoustie in 1999. Otherwise, he'd had trouble making the cut.

Now that he had shown he can play this game with anybody, what will come next? He said he had considered joining the PGA Tour, perhaps in 2002, but he would play in Europe the rest of 2001, then decide what's next.

Meanwhile, he'll savor the moment.

June 14-18, 2001, Southern Hills Country Club, Tulsa, Okla.

Contestant	Rounds				Total	Prize
Retief Goosen	66	70	69	71	276	$900,000.00
Mark Brooks	72	64	70	70	276	530,000.00
(Goosen defeated Brooks in 18-hole playoff, 70-72.)						
Stewart Cink	69	69	67	72	277	325,310.00
Rocco Mediate	71	68	67	72	278	226,777.00
Paul Azinger	74	67	69	71	281	172,912.00
Tom Kite	73	72	72	64	281	172,912.00
Angel Cabrera	70	71	72	69	282	125,172.00
Davis Love III	72	69	71	70	282	125,172.00
Phil Mickelson	70	69	68	75	282	125,172.00
Vijay Singh	74	70	74	64	282	125,172.00
Kirk Triplett	72	69	71	70	282	125,172.00
Michael Allen	77	68	67	71	283	91,734.00
Sergio Garcia	70	68	68	77	283	91,734.00
Matt Gogel	70	69	74	70	283	91,734.00
Tiger Woods	74	71	69	69	283	91,734.00
Chris DiMarco	69	73	70	72	284	75,337.00
David Duval	70	69	71	74	284	75,337.00
Scott Hoch	73	73	69	69	284	75,337.00
Corey Pavin	70	75	68	72	285	63,426.00
Chris Perry	72	71	73	69	285	63,426.00
Mike Weir	67	76	68	74	285	63,426.00
Thomas Bjorn	72	69	73	72	286	54,813.00
Scott Verplank	71	71	73	71	286	54,813.00
Olin Browne	71	74	71	71	287	42,523.00
Mark Calcavecchia	70	74	73	70	287	42,523.00
Joe Durant	71	74	70	72	287	42,523.00
Tom Lehman	76	68	69	74	287	42,523.00
Steve Lowery	71	73	72	71	287	42,523.00
Hal Sutton	70	75	71	71	287	42,523.00
Darren Clarke	74	71	71	72	288	30,055.00
Bob Estes	70	72	75	71	288	30,055.00
Padraig Harrington	73	70	71	74	288	30,055.00
Gabriel Hjertstedt	72	74	70	72	288	30,055.00
Steve Jones	73	73	72	70	288	30,055.00
J.L. Lewis	68	68	77	75	288	30,055.00
Bob May	72	72	69	75	288	30,055.00
*Bryce Molder	75	71	68	74	288	Medal
Jesper Parnevik	73	73	74	68	288	30,055.00
Dean Wilson	71	74	72	71	288	30,055.00
Briny Baird	71	72	70	76	289	23,933.00
Tim Herron	71	74	73	71	289	23,933.00
Bernhard Langer	71	73	71	74	289	23,933.00
Shaun Micheel	73	70	75	71	289	23,933.00
Tom Byrum	74	72	72	72	290	18,780.00
Brandel Chamblee	72	71	71	76	290	18,780.00
Fred Funk	78	68	71	73	290	18,780.00
Toshimitsu Izawa	69	74	74	73	290	18,780.00
Jeff Maggert	69	73	72	76	290	18,780.00

Contestant	Rounds				Total	Prize
Kevin Sutherland	73	72	73	72	290	18,780.00
Duffy Waldorf	75	68	69	78	290	18,780.00
Eduardo Romero	74	72	72	73	291	15,035.00
Jose Coceres	70	73	75	74	292	13,164.00
Scott Dunlap	74	70	73	75	292	13,164.00
Hale Irwin	67	75	74	76	292	13,164.00
Brandt Jobe	77	68	71	76	292	13,164.00
Frank Lickliter II	75	71	70	76	292	13,164.00
Colin Montgomerie	71	70	77	74	292	13,164.00
Loren Roberts	69	76	69	78	292	13,164.00
Bob Tway	75	71	72	74	292	13,164.00
Jimmy Walker	79	66	74	73	292	13,164.00
Mark Wiebe	73	72	74	73	292	13,164.00
Jim Furyk	70	70	71	82	293	11,443.00
Dudley Hart	71	73	74	75	293	11,443.00
Tim Petrovic	74	71	75	73	293	11,443.00
Richard Zokol	72	71	74	76	293	11,443.00
Ernie Els	71	74	77	72	294	10,368.00
Dan Forsman	75	71	77	71	294	10,368.00
Harrison Frazar	73	73	76	72	294	10,368.00
Peter Lonard	76	69	70	79	294	10,368.00
David Peoples	73	73	72	76	294	10,368.00
David Toms	71	71	77	75	294	10,368.00
Nick Faldo	76	70	74	75	295	9,508.00
Franklin Langham	75	71	75	74	295	9,508.00
Mathias Gronberg	74	69	74	79	296	8,863.00
Thongchai Jaidee	73	73	72	78	296	8,863.00
Anthony Kang	74	72	77	73	296	8,863.00
Gary Orr	74	72	74	76	296	8,863.00
Jim McGovern	71	73	77	76	297	8,325.00
Stephen Gangluff	74	72	78	77	301	8,105.00

Rich Beem	74	73	147	Steve Flesch	81	69	150	*John Harris	76	77	153
Chad Campbell	76	71	147	Chris Gonzales	75	75	150	Brian Henninger	75	78	153
Robert Damron	73	74	147	Tripp Isenhour	73	77	150	Kevin Johnson	77	76	153
Brad Faxon	73	74	147	Miguel Angel Jimenez	77	73	150	Michael Campbell	77	77	154
Mike Hulbert	75	72	147	Paul Lawrie	73	77	150	Stuart Appleby	80	75	155
Lee Janzen	77	70	147	Joey Maxon	74	76	150	Ben Bates	75	80	155
Pete Jordan	77	70	147	Jay Don Blake	75	76	151	Carlos Franco	76	79	155
Gary Koch	75	72	147	Todd Fischer	76	75	151	Jeff Hart	80	75	155
Tom Pernice, Jr.	74	73	147	Paul Goydos	76	75	151	Scott Johnson	82	73	155
Brett Quigley	71	76	147	Donnie Hammond	76	75	151	John Maginnes	79	76	155
K.J. Choi	78	70	148	John Huston	75	76	151	Dicky Pride	77	78	155
Robert Gamez	74	74	148	Joel Kribel	74	77	151	*Jeff Quinney	82	73	155
Skip Kendall	74	74	148	Justin Leonard	78	73	151	Chris Anderson	77	79	156
Mark O'Meara	74	74	148	Mike Sposa	78	73	151	Notah Begay III	78	78	156
Dennis Paulson	75	73	148	Esteban Toledo	74	77	151	Clark Dennis	79	77	156
Nick Price	74	74	148	Lee Westwood	75	76	151	Wes Heffernan	77	79	156
Steve Stricker	73	75	148	Jess Daley	80	72	152	Willie Wood	75	81	156
Robert Allenby	74	75	149	John Douma	77	75	152	Marty Schiene	78	79	157
Billy Andrade	75	74	149	Jason Dufner	74	78	152	Jeff Barlow	78	81	159
Charles Howell	75	74	149	Jeff Freeman	77	75	152	Chris Wall	81	79	160
Jose Maria Olazabal	77	72	149	Shingo Katayama	77	75	152	George Frake II	84	77	161
Carl Paulson	73	76	149	Brad Klapprott	75	77	152	Phil Price			WD
Toru Taniguchi	78	71	149	Gary Nicklaus	78	74	152	Jarmo Sandelin		72	WD
Ronnie Black	76	74	150	Charles Raulerson, Jr.	77	75	152	Jay Williamson		75	DQ
Kyle Blackman	74	76	150	Chris Smith	74	78	152	Pierre Fulke		76	WD
Fred Couples	76	74	150	Glen Day	77	76	153				

Professionals not returning 72-hole scores received $1,000 each.   *Denotes amateur.

101st U.S. OPEN Statistics

Hole	1	2	3	4	5	6	7	8	9	10	11	12	13	14	15	16	17	18	Total	
Par	4	4	4	4	5	3	4	3	4	4	3	4	5	3	4	4	4	4	70	
Retief Goosen																				
Round 1	③	③	4	4	5	3	③	②	③	4	3	4	④	3	4	5	5	4	66	
Round 2	4	4	4	4	5	3	4	3	4	4	3	4	④	4	4	4	③	5	70	
Round 3	4	4	4	③	5	3	5	3	③	4	3	4	5	3	4	4	4	4	69	
Round 4	4	4	4	4	5	②	4	4	5	③	3	4	5	4	③	4	4	5	71	276
Playoff	4	4	4	4	5	②	4	3	③	③	3	5	5	3	4	4	5	5	70	
Mark Brooks																				
Round 1	4	4	4	4	6	3	4	3	4	4	②	4	5	3	4	4	4	6	72	
Round 2	③	③	4	③	④	②	4	3	4	4	②	4	5	3	4	4	4	4	64	
Round 3	4	5	③	4	6	3	4	3	4	4	3	4	5	3	③	4	4	4	70	
Round 4	4	4	4	4	6	3	4	3	4	4	②	4	④	3	4	4	4	5	70	276
Playoff	4	4	③	4	5	3	5	3	5	5	3	5	5	3	4	4	③	4	72	
Stewart Cink																				
Round 1	5	4	4	4	④	3	4	5	5	4	②	4	5	3	③	③	4	③	69	
Round 2	5	4	4	4	④	②	4	3	4	4	3	4	5	4	③	4	4	4	69	
Round 3	5	6	4	③	④	②	③	3	4	4	3	4	④	3	③	4	4	4	67	
Round 4	4	4	4	4	6	3	4	3	4	4	②	4	6	3	4	4	③	6	72	277

○ Circled numbers represent birdies or eagles.   □ Squared numbers represent bogeys or worse.

Hole	Yards	Par	Eagles	Birdies	Pars	Bogeys	Double Bogeys	Higher	Average
1	454	4	0	48	284	119	14	0	4.213
2	467	4	0	31	262	133	35	4	4.396
3	408	4	0	56	299	95	14	1	4.151
4	368	4	0	62	292	102	9	0	4.125
5	642	5	0	65	264	125	9	2	5.181
6	175	3	1	59	344	56	5	0	3.011
7	382	4	0	59	315	84	7	0	4.084
8	225	3	0	25	297	135	8	0	3.271
9	374	4	0	60	274	114	16	1	4.191
OUT	3,495	35	1	465	2,631	963	117	8	36.623
10	374	4	1	57	298	98	11	0	4.131
11	165	3	1	82	291	84	7	0	3.030
12	456	4	0	45	269	122	27	2	4.295
13	534	5	10	138	251	59	6	1	4.819
14	215	3	0	42	283	132	8	0	3.228
15	412	4	0	51	251	141	21	1	4.290
16	491	4	0	27	270	154	12	2	4.340
17	365	4	0	70	299	87	9	0	4.075
18	466	4	0	28	233	177	25	2	4.441
IN	3,478	35	12	540	2,445	1,054	126	8	36.649
TOTAL	6,973	70	13	1,005	5,076	2,017	243	16	73.272

101st U.S. Open Past Results

Date	Winner	Score	Runner-Up	Venue
1895	Horace Rawlins	173 - 36 holes	Willie Dunn	Newport GC, Newport, RI
1896	James Foulis	152 - 36 holes	Horace Rawlins	Shinnecock Hills GC, Southampton, NY
1897	Joe Lloyd	162 - 36 holes	Willie Anderson	Chicago GC, Wheaton, IL
1898	Fred Herd	328 - 72 holes	Alex Smith	Myopia Hunt Club, S. Hamilton, MA
1899	Willie Smith	315	George Low Val Fitzjohn W.H. Way	Baltimore CC, Baltimore, MD
1900	Harry Vardon	313	J.H. Taylor	Chicago GC, Wheaton, IL
1901	*Willie Anderson (85)	331	Alex Smith (86)	Myopia Hunt Club, S. Hamilton, MA
1902	Laurie Auchterlonie	307	Stewart Gardner	Garden City GC, Garden City, NY
1903	*Willie Anderson (82)	307	David Brown (84)	Baltusrol GC, Springfield, NJ
1904	Willie Anderson	303	Gil Nicholls	Glen View Club, Golf, IL
1905	Willie Anderson	314	Alex Smith	Myopia Hunt Club, S. Hamilton, MA
1906	Alex Smith	295	Willie Smith	Onwentsia Club, Lake Forest, IL
1907	Alex Ross	302	Gil Nicholls	Philadelphia Cricket Club, Chestnut Hill, PA
1908	*Fred McLeod (77)	322	Willie Smith (83)	Myopia Hunt Club, S. Hamilton, MA
1909	George Sargent	290	Tom McNamara	Englewood GC, Englewood, NJ
1910	*Alex Smith (71) Macdonald Smith (77)	298	John J. McDermott (75)	Philadelphia Cricket Club, Chestnut Hill, PA
1911	*John J. McDermott (80)	307	Michael J. Brady (82) George O. Simpson (85)	Chicago GC, Wheaton, IL
1912	John J. McDermott	294	Tom McNamara	CC of Buffalo, Buffalo, NY
1913	*Francis Ouimet (72)	304	Harry Vardon (77) Edward Ray (78)	The Country Club, Brookline, MA
1914	Walter Hagen	290	Charles Evans, Jr.	Midlothian CC, Blue Island, IL
1915	Jerome D. Travers	297	Tom McNamara	Baltusrol GC, Springfield, NJ
1916	Charles Evans, Jr.	286	Jock Hutchinson	Minikahda Club, Minneapolis, MN
1917-18	No Championships Played — World War I			
1919	*Walter Hagen (77)	301	Michael J. Brady (78)	Brae Burn CC, West Newton, MA
1920	Edward Ray	295	Harry Vardon Jack Burke, Sr. Leo Diegel Jock Hutchison	Inverness Club, Toledo, OH
1921	James M. Barnes	289	Walter Hagen Fred McLeod	Columbia CC, Chevy Chase, MD
1922	Gene Sarazen	288	John L. Black Robert T. Jones, Jr.	Skokie CC, Glencoe, IL
1923	*Robert T. Jones, Jr. (76)	296	Bobby Cruickshank (78)	Inwood CC, Inwood, NY
1924	Cyril Walker	297	Robert T. Jones, Jr.	Oakland Hills CC, Birmingham, MI
1925	*William MacFarlane (147)	291	Robert T. Jones, Jr. (148)	Worcester CC, Worcester, MA
1926	Robert T. Jones, Jr.	293	Joe Turnesa	Scioto CC, Columbus, OH
1927	*Tommy Armour (76)	301	Harry Cooper (79)	Oakmont CC, Oakmont, PA
1928	*Johnny Farrell (143)	294	Robert T. Jones, Jr. (144)	Olympia Fields CC, Matteson, IL
1929	*Robert T. Jones, Jr. (141)	294	Al Espinosa (164)	Winged Foot GC, Mamaroneck, NY
1930	Robert T. Jones, Jr.	287	Macdonald Smith	Interlachen CC, Hopkins, MN

Past Results

Date	Winner	Score	Runner-Up	Venue
1931	*Billy Burke (149-148)	292	George Von Elm (149-149)	Inverness Club, Toledo, OH
1932	Gene Sarazen	286	Phil Perkins Bobby Cruickshank	Fresh Meadows CC, Flushing, NY
1933	Johnny Goodman	287	Ralph Guldahl	North Shore CC, Glenview, IL
1934	Olin Dutra	293	Gene Sarazen	Merion Cricket Club, Ardmore, PA
1935	Sam Parks, Jr.	299	Jimmy Thomson	Oakmont CC, Oakmont, PA
1936	Tony Manero	282	Harry Cooper	Baltusrol GC, Springfield, NJ
1937	Ralph Guldahl	281	Sam Snead	Oakland Hills CC, Birmingham, MI
1938	Ralph Guldahl	284	Dick Metz	Cherry Hills CC, Englewood, CO
1939	*Byron Nelson (68-70)	284	Craig Wood (68-73) Denny Shute (76)	Philadelphia CC, West Conshohocken, PA
1940	*Lawson Little (70)	287	Gene Sarazen (73)	Canterbury GC, Cleveland, OH
1941	Craig Wood	284	Denny Shute	Colonial Club, Fort Worth, TX
1942-45	No Championships Played — World War II			
1946	*Lloyd Mangrum (72-72)	284	Vic Ghezzi (72-73) Byron Nelson (72-73)	Canterbury GC, Cleveland, OH
1947	*Lew Worsham (69)	282	Sam Snead (70)	St. Louis CC, Clayton, MO
1948	Ben Hogan	276	Jimmy Demaret	Riviera CC, Los Angeles, CA
1949	Cary Middlecoff	286	Sam Snead Clayton Heafner	Medinah CC, Medinah, IL
1950	*Ben Hogan (69)	287	Lloyd Mangrum (73) George Fazio (75)	Merion GC, Ardmore, PA
1951	Ben Hogan	287	Clayton Heafner	Oakland Hills CC, Birmingham, MI
1952	Julius Boros	281	Ed (Porky) Oliver	Northwood CC, Dallas, TX
1953	Ben Hogan	283	Sam Snead	Oakmont CC, Oakmont, PA
1954	Ed Furgol	284	Gene Littler	Baltusrol GC, Springfield, NJ
1955	*Jack Fleck (69)	287	Ben Hogan (72)	The Olympic Club, San Francisco, CA
1956	Cary Middlecoff	281	Ben Hogan Julius Boros	Oak Hill CC, Rochester, NY
1957	*Dick Mayer (72)	282	Cary Middlecoff (79)	Inverness Club, Toledo, OH
1958	Tommy Bolt	283	Gary Player	Southern Hills CC, Tulsa, OK
1959	Billy Casper	282	Bob Rosburg	Winged Foot GC, Mamaroneck, NY
1960	Arnold Palmer	280	Jack Nicklaus	Cherry Hills CC, Englewood, CO
1961	Gene Littler	281	Bob Goalby Doug Sanders	Oakland Hills CC, Birmingham, MI
1962	*Jack Nicklaus (71)	283	Arnold Palmer (74)	Oakmont CC, Oakmont, PA
1963	*Julius Boros (70)	293	Jacky Cupit (73) Arnold Palmer (76)	The Country Club, Brookline, MA
1964	Ken Venturi	278	Tommy Jacobs	Congressional CC, Bethesda, MD
1965	*Gary Player (71)	282	Kel Nagle (74)	Bellerive CC, St. Louis, MO
1966	*Billy Casper (69)	278	Arnold Palmer (73)	The Olympic Club, San Francisco, CA
1967	Jack Nicklaus	275	Arnold Palmer	Baltusrol GC, Springfield, NJ
1968	Lee Trevino	275	Jack Nicklaus	Oak Hill CC, Rochester, NY
1969	Orville Moody	281	Deane Beman Al Geiberger Bob Rosburg	Champions GC, Houston, TX
1970	Tony Jacklin	281	Dave Hill	Hazeltine National GC, Chaska, MN
1971	*Lee Trevino (68)	280	Jack Nicklaus (71)	Merion GC, Ardmore, PA
1972	Jack Nicklaus	290	Bruce Crampton	Pebble Beach GL, Pebble Beach, CA
1973	Johnny Miller	279	John Schlee	Oakmont CC, Oakmont, PA
1974	Hale Irwin	287	Forrest Fezler	Winged Foot GC, Mamaroneck, NY
1975	*Lou Graham (71)	287	John Mahaffey (73)	Medinah CC, Medinah, IL
1976	Jerry Pate	277	Tom Weiskopf Al Geiberger	Atlanta Athletic Club, Duluth, GA

Date	Winner	Score	Runner-Up	Venue
1977	Hubert Green	278	Lou Graham	Southern Hills CC, Tulsa, OK
1978	Andy North	285	Dave Stockton J.C. Snead	Cherry Hills CC, Englewood, CO
1979	Hale Irwin	284	Gary Player Jerry Pate	Inverness Club, Toledo, OH
1980	Jack Nicklaus	272	Isao Aoki	Baltusrol GC, Springfield, NJ
1981	David Graham	273	George Burns Bill Rogers	Merion GC, Ardmore, PA
1982	Tom Watson	282	Jack Nicklaus	Pebble Beach GL, Pebble Beach, CA
1983	Larry Nelson	280	Tom Watson	Oakmont CC, Oakmont, PA
1984	*Fuzzy Zoeller (67)	276	Greg Norman (75)	Winged Foot GC, Mamaroneck, NY
1985	Andy North	279	Dave Barr Chen Tze Chung Denis Watson	Oakland Hills CC, Birmingham, MI
1986	Raymond Floyd	279	Lanny Wadkins Chip Beck	Shinnecock Hills GC, Southampton, NY
1987	Scott Simpson	277	Tom Watson	The Olympic Club, San Francisco, CA
1988	*Curtis Strange (71)	278	Nick Faldo (75)	The Country Club, Brookline, MA
1989	Curtis Strange	278	Chip Beck Mark McCumber Ian Woosnam	Oak Hill CC, Rochester, NY
1990	*Hale Irwin (74+3)	280	Mike Donald (74+4)	Medinah CC, Medinah, IL
1991	*Payne Stewart (75)	282	Scott Simpson (77)	Hazeltine National GC, Chaska, MN
1992	Tom Kite	285	Jeff Sluman	Pebble Beach GL, Pebble Beach, CA
1993	Lee Janzen	272	Payne Stewart	Baltusrol GC, Springfield, NJ
1994	*Ernie Els (74+4+4)	279	Loren Roberts (74+4+5) Colin Montgomerie (78)	Oakmont CC, Oakmont, PA
1995	Corey Pavin	280	Greg Norman	Shinnecock Hills GC, Southampton, NY
1996	Steve Jones	278	Tom Lehman Davis Love III	Oakland Hills CC, Birmingham, MI
1997	Ernie Els	276	Colin Montgomerie	Congressional CC, Bethesda, MD
1998	Lee Janzen	280	Payne Stewart	The Olympic Club, San Francisco, CA
1999	Payne Stewart	279	Phil Mickelson	Pinehurst No. 2, Pinehurst, NC
2000	Tiger Woods	272	Miguel Angel Jimenez Ernie Els	Pebble Beach GL, Pebble Beach, CA
2001	*Retief Goosen (70)	276	Mark Brooks (72)	Southern Hills CC, Tulsa, OK

*Winner in playoff; figures in parentheses indicate scores

101st U.S. OPEN Championship Records

Oldest champion (years/months/days)
45/0/15 — Hale Irwin (1990)

Youngest champion
19/10/14 — John J. McDermott (1911)

Most victories
4 — Willie Anderson (1901, '03, '04, '05)
4 — Robert T. Jones, Jr. (1923, '26, '29, '30)
4 — Ben Hogan (1948, '50, '51, '53)
4 — Jack Nicklaus (1962, '67, '72, '80)
3 — Hale Irwin (1974, '79, '90)
2 — by 14 players: Alex Smith (1906, '10), John J. McDermott (1911, '12), Walter Hagen (1914, '19), Gene Sarazen (1922, '32), Ralph Guldahl (1937, '38), Cary Middlecoff (1949, '56), Julius Boros (1952, '63), Billy Casper (1959, '66), Lee Trevino (1968, '71), Andy North (1978, '85), Curtis Strange (1988, '89), Ernie Els (1994, '97), Lee Janzen (1993, '98), and Payne Stewart (1991, '99).

Consecutive victories
Willie Anderson (1903, '04, '05)
John J. McDermott (1911, '12)
Robert T. Jones, Jr. (1929, '30)
Ralph Guldahl (1937, '38)
Ben Hogan (1950, '51)
Curtis Strange (1988, '89)

Most times runner-up
4 — Sam Snead
4 — Robert T. Jones, Jr.
4 — Arnold Palmer
4 — Jack Nicklaus

Longest course
7,213 yards — Congressional CC, Bethesda, MD (1997)

Shortest course
Since World War II
6,528 yards — Merion GC (East Course), Ardmore, PA (1971, '81)

Most often host club of Open
7 — Baltusrol GC, Springfield, NJ (1903, '15, '36, '54, '67, '80, '93)
7 — Oakmont (PA) CC (1927, '35, '53, '62, '73, '83, '94)

Largest entry
8,457 (2000)

Smallest entry
11 (1895)

Lowest score, 72 holes
272 — Jack Nicklaus (63-71-70-68), at Baltusrol GC (Lower Course), Springfield, NJ (1980)
272 — Lee Janzen (67-67-69-69), at Baltusrol GC (Lower Course), Springfield, NJ (1993)
272 — Tiger Woods (65-69-71-67), at Pebble Beach GL, Pebble Beach, CA (2000)

Lowest score, first 54 holes
203 — George Burns (69-66-68), at Merion GC (East Course), Ardmore, PA (1981)
203 — Tze-Chung Chen (65-69-69), at Oakland Hills CC (South Course), Birmingham, MI (1985)
203 — Lee Janzen (67-67-69), at Baltusrol GC (Lower Course), Springfield, NJ (1993)

Lowest score, last 54 holes
203 — Loren Roberts (69-64-70), at Oakmont CC, Oakmont, PA (1994)

Lowest score, first 36 holes
134 — Jack Nicklaus (63-71), at Baltusrol GC (Lower Course), Springfield, NJ (1980)
134 — Chen Tze-Chung (65-69), at Oakland Hills CC (South Course), Birmingham, MI (1985)
134 — Lee Janzen (67-67), at Baltusrol GC (Lower Course), Springfield, NJ (1993)
134 — Tiger Woods (65-69), at Pebble Beach GL, Pebble Beach, CA (2000)

Lowest score, last 36 holes
132 — Larry Nelson (65-67), at Oakmont CC, Oakmont, PA (1983)

Lowest score, 9 holes
29 — Neal Lancaster (second nine, fourth round) at Shinnecock Hills GC, Southampton, NY (1995)
29 — Neal Lancaster (second nine, second round) at Oakland Hills CC, Birmingham, MI (1996)

Lowest score, 18 holes
63 — Johnny Miller, fourth round at Oakmont CC, Oakmont, PA (1973)
63 — Jack Nicklaus, first round at Baltusrol GC (Lower Course), Springfield, NJ (1980)
63 — Tom Weiskopf, first round at Baltusrol GC (Lower Course), Springfield, NJ (1980)

Largest winning margin
15 — Tiger Woods (272), at Pebble Beach GL, Pebble Beach CA (2000)

Highest winning score
Since World War II
293 — Julius Boros, at The Country Club, Brookline, MA (1963) (won in playoff)

Best start by champion
63 — Jack Nicklaus, at Baltusrol GC (Lower Course), Springfield, NJ (1980)

Best finish by champion
63 — Johnny Miller, at Oakmont (PA) CC (1973)

Worst start by champion
Since World War II
76 — Ben Hogan, at Oakland Hills CC (South Course), Birmingham, MI (1951)

76 — Jack Fleck, at The Olympic Club (Lake Course), San Francisco, CA (1955)

Worst finish by champion
Since World War II
75 — Cary Middlecoff, at Medinah CC (No. 3 Course), Medinah, IL (1949)
75 — Hale Irwin, at Inverness Club, Toledo, OH (1979)

Lowest score to lead field, 18 holes
63 — Jack Nicklaus and Tom Weiskopf, at Baltusrol GC (Lower Course), Springfield, NJ (1980)

Lowest score to lead field, 36 holes
134 — Jack Nicklaus (63-71), at Baltusrol GC (Lower Course), Springfield, NJ (1980)
134 — Chen Tze-Chung (65-69), at Oakland Hills CC (South Course), Birmingham, MI (1985)
134 — Lee Janzen (67-67), at Baltusrol GC (Lower Course), Springfield, NJ (1993)
134 — Tiger Woods (65-69), at Pebble Beach GL, Pebble Beach, CA (2000)

Lowest score to lead field, 54 holes
203 — George Burns (69-66-68), at Merion GC (East Course), Ardmore, PA (1981)
203 — Chen Tze-Chung (65-69-69), at Oakland Hills CC (South Course), Birmingham, MI (1985)
203 — Lee Janzen (67-67-69), at Baltusrol GC (Lower Course), Springfield, NJ (1993)

Highest score to lead field, 18 holes
Since World War II
71 — Sam Snead, at Oakland Hills CC (South Course), Birmingham, MI (1951)
71 — Tommy Bolt, Julius Boros, and Dick Metz, at Southern Hills CC, Tulsa, OK (1958)
71 — Tony Jacklin, at Hazeltine National GC, Chaska, MN (1970)
71 — Orville Moody, Jack Nicklaus, Chi Chi Rodriguez, Mason Rudolph, Tom Shaw, and Kermit Zarley, at Pebble Beach (CA) Golf Links (1972)

Highest score to lead field, 36 holes
Since World War II
144 — Bobby Locke (73-71), at Oakland Hills CC (South Course), Birmingham, MI (1951)
144 — Tommy Bolt (67-77) and E. Harvie Ward (74-70), at The Olympic Club (Lake Course), San Francisco, CA (1955)
144 — Homero Blancas (74-70), Bruce Crampton (74-70), Jack Nicklaus (71-73), Cesar Seduno (72-72), Lanny Wadkins (76-68) and Kermit Zarley (71-73), at Pebble Beach (CA) Golf Links (1972)

Highest score to lead field, 54 holes
Since World War II
218 — Bobby Locke (73-71-74), at Oakland Hills CC (South Course), Birmingham, MI (1951)
218 — Jacky Cupit (70-72-76), at The Country Club, Brookline, MA (1963)

Highest 36-hole cut
155 — at The Olympic Club (Lakeside Course), San Francisco, CA (1955)

Most players to tie for lead, 18 holes
7 — at Pebble Beach (CA) Golf Links (1972); at Southern Hills CC, Tulsa, OK (1977); and at Shinnecock Hills GC, Southampton, NY (1896)

Most players to tie for lead, 36 holes
6 — at Pebble Beach (CA) Golf Links (1972)

Most players to tie for lead, 54 holes
4 — at Oakmont (PA) CC (1973)

Most sub-par rounds, championship
124 — at Medinah CC (No. 3 Course), Medinah, IL (1990)

Most sub-par 72-hole totals, championship
28 — at Medinah CC (No. 3 Course), Medinah, IL (1990)

Most sub-par scores, first round
39 — at Medinah CC (No. 3 Course), Medinah, IL (1990)

Most sub-par scores, second round
47 — at Medinah CC (No. 3 Course), Medinah, IL (1990)

Most sub-par scores, third round
24 — at Medinah CC (No. 3 Course), Medinah, IL (1990)

Most sub-par scores, fourth round
18 — at Baltusrol GC (Lower Course), Springfield, NJ (1993)

Most sub-par rounds by one player in one championship
4 — Billy Casper, at The Olympic Club (Lakeside Course), San Francisco, CA (1966)
4 — Lee Trevino, at Oak Hill CC (East Course), Rochester, NY (1968)
4 — Tony Jacklin, at Hazeltine National GC, Chaska, MN (1970)
4 — Lee Janzen, at Baltusrol GC (Lower Course), Springfield, NJ (1993)

Highest score, one hole
19 — Ray Ainsley, at the 16th (par 4) at Cherry Hills CC, Englewood, CO (1938)

Most consecutive birdies
6 — George Burns (holes 2–7), at Pebble Beach (CA) Golf Links (1972) and Andy Dillard (holes 1-6), at Pebble Beach (CA) Golf Links (1992)

Most consecutive 3s
7 — Hubert Green (holes 10–16), at Southern Hills Country Club, Tulsa, OK (1977)
7 — Peter Jacobsen (holes 1–7), at The Country Club, Brookline, MA (1988)

Most consecutive Opens
44 — Jack Nicklaus (1957-2000)

Most Opens completed 72 holes
35 — Jack Nicklaus

Most consecutive Opens completed 72 holes
22 — Walter Hagen (1913-36; no Championships 1917-18)
22 — Gene Sarazen (1920-41)
22 — Gary Player (1958-79)

Robert Sommers is the former editor and publisher of the USGA's *Golf Journal*, author of *The U.S. Open: Golf's Ultimate Challenge* and *Golf Anecdotes*. He is based in Port St. Lucie, Fla.

Michael Cohen is a photographer based in New York City and a contributor to many magazines and books.

Sam Greenwood is a photographer based in Ponte Vedra Beach, Fla., and a contributor to many publications.

Par and Yardage

Hole	Par	Yardage	Hole	Par	Yardage
1	4	454	10	4	374
2	4	467	11	3	165
3	4	408	12	4	456
4	4	368	13	5	534
5	5	642	14	3	215
6	3	175	15	4	412
7	4	382	16	4	491
8	3	225	17	4	365
9	4	374	18	4	466
	35	3,495		35	3,478
				70	6,973